THE STORY OF AN AFRICAN VILLAGE

THE STORY OF AN AFRICAN VILLAGE

Robert Peprah-Gyamfi

Perseverance Books
Loughborough, UK

THE STORY OF AN AFRICAN VILLAGE
First published in 2010 under the title
GROWING UP IN A SMALL AFRICAN VILLAGE

All Rights Reserved. Copyright © 2014 Robert Peprah-Gyamfi

No part of this book may be reproduced or transmitted in any form or by any means, graphic, electronic, or mechanical, including photocopying, recording, taping or by any information storage or retrieval system, without the permission in writing from the publisher.

PERSEVERANCE BOOKS

For information address:
PERSEVERANCE BOOKS
P.O. BOX 8505
LOUGHBOROUGH
LE11 9BZ
UK

www.peprah-gyamfi.com

ISBN: 978-0-9570780-6-2

To the inhabitants of tiny Mpintimpi, the village in Ghana where my eyes first saw the light of day, past, present and future.

TABLE OF CONTENTS

Preface ix
Introduction xi
Prologue: Do Not Forget Us xiii
1 A Tourist's Guide to Mpintimpi 1
2 The Arduous Journey of the New Arrival to Our Home 15
3 Recruiting for the Academic Journey 18
4 The Tedious Walk to and From School 21
5 Flies and Bees Disturbing the Morning Assembly 24
6 The Young Academic on the Point of Explosion 27
7 The Awful Experience with the Red-Hot Iron 29
8 The Call to Discipline and the Need to Improvise 31
9 Call it Child Labour if You Will! 33
10 The School Feast and the Day of Reckoning 35
11 My Cousin the Driver 37
12 The Village News Broadcaster and the Naughty Children 38
13 Joining Forces for the Common Good 40
14 The Treachery of the Farmer's Kids Exposed 42
15 The Tree that Produces Black Gold 47
16 The Tree with a Thousand and One Uses 52
17 One Fruit, Two Edible Oils 55
18 Simple Peasants Cracking Complicated Chemical Formulas 57
19 The Iron Lady of Mpintimpi 59
20 "Kill Me Quick!" 61
21 The Thief that Strikes from Above 63
22 Our Audacious Four-Legged Companions 65
23 My Uncle, the Professional Hunter 67

24 The Expert Grasscutters and the Rats from Gambia.......................69
25 The Biting Scissors and the Crawling Beings................................72
26 Be on the Lookout for the Angry Snakes! 75
27 Ordinary and Extraordinary Fishing Methods 77
28 Please Forgive Our Ignorance...79
29 Wild Honey for Breakfast 82
30 Enemas and Suppositories 'Made in Mpintimpi'...........................83
31 Heating Legs Over Boiling Pots for a Cure 87
32 Self-Made Dispensers 89
33 Quack Doctors and 'Smuggle Injections' 91
34 Dealing with Three Medical Emergencies......................................93
35 Our Friend from Above...97
36 Our Friend by Night..99
37 "Some are Comfortably Seated While Others are
   Suffering in Their Seats"..101
38 A Curious Boxing Match on the Streets of Mpintimpi 103
39 A Welcome Change to a Dull Evening Routine.............................106
40 The Drivers' Assistants and the Cheeky Village Boys..................108
41 The Health Inspector and the Unkept Armpit 112
42 Flee the Taxman if You Can! 115
43 A Few Pots of Palm Wine for Differences Settled........................116
44 My Senior Brother and the Neighbour's Daughter.......................119
45 The Sad End to a Promising Romance 123
46 The Wailing Grandchildren...125
47 A Rare Tragic Happening in a Serene Environment.....................127
48 Abandoned Wheel Rims as Church Bells.....................................130
49 Christmas Carols for Biscuits 132
50 Pocket Money Earned the Hard Way 134
51 The Tragic End of 'Poor No Friend' 137
52 The Vociferous Wives and the Aging Footballers........................139
53 First the Sweat then the Balls...143
54 Double Tragedy Around the Bathroom...146
55 A Peculiar Method of Battery-Charging 148
56 Those Who Share Their Last Pins with Their Neighbours 151
57 For Credit Come Tomorrow..152

58 Unconventional Saving's Banks and Thumb-Printed
Agreements 156
59 "They Say I Have TB!" 159
60 Apollo 11 Wreaks Havoc on the Streets of Tiny Mpintimpi.........162
61 Table Salt for a Vote Cast..165
62 The Young Traveller Who Missed His Mother's Kitchen 168
63 "Eyes are Red When Things are Bad!" 171
64 The Village Boy Goes to Town 174
65 Do Not Forget Us Still 179
Epilogue: GHANA 2 USA 1 180

PREFACE

FOR ANYONE growing up in the West—in Europe, America or Canada, for instance—this fascinating book will be an eye opener. Many Western readers may well have been born in the sterile conditions of a modern hospital, with the advantages of technology and midwives and doctors on tap, in smart white uniforms and coats, all with a sound background of diplomas and university degrees. And as they grew up, they were nurtured by the comforts and benefits of mod cons, of television sets, radios, computers; if they became ill, a doctor was probably in easy reach, through a home visit or a visit to the accident and emergency ward, and in the worst case scenario, by means of an ambulance by dint of dialling 999 (or 911).

Not so in Mpintimpi, that small village in rural Ghana, isolated from modern facilities, where the only means of reaching a hospital, let alone a qualified doctor, was by hitching a lift on a crowded lorry on muddy or potholed roads. That was the least of the villagers' worries, the main problem being the lack of money, and the absence of medical insurance, which would make medical treatment affordable. Consequently many people there resorted to witch doctors, or amateur herbalists, or self-styled 'doctors' who went around administering crude injections!

In spite of the severe difficulties encountered by the author who grew up in little Mpintimpi—not just medical, but educational (the absence of schools, for example), and horticultural (based entirely on a subsistence economy)—he has given us, here, a delightful insight into a different way of life. In spite of the severe hardships, there was the overwhelming love and concern that existed in the network of extended families, who, if they were to survive at all, had to care for one another, and assist one another in the daily grind of life. His book conjures up a picture of genuine human values that should underlie any society, and which, regrettably, no longer underpin the many sophisticated societies of our Western world, now being eroded by drugs, immorality and atheism. We may have the hospitals, the qualified doctors, the technological equipment, the universities, the sterile buildings of glass and chrome—but do we have that basic human bond, that cooperative spirit, that made Mpintimpi the gem of human compassion that it was?

Charles Muller
MA (Wales), PhD (London), D.Litt (UFS), D.Ed (SA)

INTRODUCTION

IN JULY 1988, while a fourth year medical student at the Hanover Medical School in Northern Germany, I went to my native Ghana to do electives in various hospitals.

Also travelling to Ghana for the same purpose was my companion, Angelika, a German national. Prior to my departure and with the kind assistance of my good friend Reverend Gottfried Kawalla, then Superintendent Minister of the Hanover- North district of the local German Lutheran Church, I raised enough funds to purchase a considerable amount of basic medication—anti-malarials, anti-diarrhoea tablets, antibiotics, painkillers, etc.—for further distribution in Ghana.

Angelika accompanied me on a visit to Mpintimpi. The news of the arrival of the 'doctors' from Germany soon spread not only throughout the little village, but to the neighbouring villages. Soon individuals with all sorts of medical conditions began to pour into our home. As Ransford, my senior brother who was accompanying us on the journey, put it, they had been hiding their diseases for lack of the means to travel to hospital.

What were we to do? Send them away with words like "We are not yet doctors, we are only fourth year medical students"!? How could they understand this, when in real life individuals less qualified than ourselves, so-called quack doctors and dispensers, were roaming about the countryside treating them?

Armed with our stethoscopes, the medication we took along and our textbooks, we did our best to treat the cases brought to us—in the main malaria, diarrhoea, abdominal discomfort, waist and joint pains. Some of them had indeed been 'hiding' their diseases, which had reached advanced clinical stages. Since they did not have the means to do so, we had to dip deep into our pockets to donate the money they needed to attend hospital.

Before that experience, I had already harboured the idea of establishing a hospital in that area to cater for the poor and needy. The fresh encounter with the medical needs of the villagers brought the urgency of the need for such a facility even closer home to me.

On my return to Germany, I put my concept of the proposed hospital on paper and launched an appeal for funds towards the realisation of my goal. Though the response was encouraging, the money raised was miles away from what was needed, leading me, at least in the interim, to bury my plan in the sand.

More than twenty years on, I am still carrying my cherished vision of a hospital that will serve not only the wealthy in society, but those who are so impoverished that they are unable to pay for their treatment. That is part of the reason why I have over the last several weeks spent long hours, sometimes deep into the night, to recount and put to paper the experiences I had growing up under the conditions prevailing in my beloved village. In this way my hope is that the whole world will know how hard it is for residents there to make ends meet, and to have some idea of their daily struggle to survive.

PROLOGUE
DO NOT FORGET US

ONE EVENING in September 1971 a young teenager dressed in khaki shorts and a black T-shirt went round the little settlement where he had spent almost all of his young life to inform the inhabitants about an impending journey that would result in his absence from the village for several weeks. Those strange to the environment he grew up in wondered why he needed to share this information with the rest of the community. After all, it was something that concerned him and his parents only. Well, in the little village almost everybody, from the very elderly to the very young, knew one another. That's why the boy's absence would be noticed within a matter of days.

"I have not seen Kofi for a while. What is wrong with him?" one or another member of the community would inquire from his parents or siblings.

"He has left for the boarding school!"

"Indeed!"

"Yes."

"To go where?"

"Akim Oda."

"And he did not consider it necessary to inform me about it? That is not a sign of good neighbourliness!"

To avoid such a situation his parents sent him on a round through the entire settlement. In whichever home he arrived, he greeted the residents politely.

"I have come to inform you that I have gained admission to college." (The villagers referred to any institution above the level of an elementary school simply as 'college'.)

"Congratulations! Which college?"

"Oda Secondary School."

"I am very proud of you! Do not let your parents down, Kofi. Learn hard to become somebody someday."

"I will do my best."

From there, he moved on to the next compound and then to the next, *and* the next, until he had spread the news to every nook and corner of the little village.

Even as he writes of his experience of growing up in the little village with the big name Mpintimpi, the words of Maame Adwoa Fante (Maame is 'Madam' in his native Twi language) still resound in his memory:

"Kofi, do not let your parents down! Instead, learn hard to attain great laurels in life. As you are aware, hardly anyone here can read and write. We did not get the opportunity you have been offered as a result of the free education policy of the Government of our newly independent country. So take advantage of the opportunity and learn hard to become somebody in life."

"Thank you very much for your advice", he replied. "I will do my best."

"You are a brilliant chap; with hard work and dedication to your books, you will surely make it."

"Thanks for your kind words."

"When that day comes, do not forget us! Yes, do not care only for your wife and kids. Think also about us; for we have all shared in the challenges that living in such a deprived community entails."

"Do not forget us!"

How often does the author of these lines think about those words! Indeed, how much he wishes he could help raise the standard of living of residents of the village where his eyes first saw the light of day—yes, the village that would prove to be a lasting influence on his life and his journey out of poverty. Easier said than done; for much as he would like to bless all of those village folk with a hospital or health centre that would provide them with medical care, affordable not only to the well-to-do, but also to the very poor, the hard realities of this life have so far prevented him from realising that goal.

In one sense, however, he is able to fulfil his goal of uplifting their condition. At least by means of this account, he is helping to bring their plight before the rest of the world. He would consider this duty as a duty to *his own*. It may not be the way he had envisaged it, but at least by means of his writing, as an author, he can ensure that his people are not forgotten—and in this way his goal is, at least, partially fulfilled.

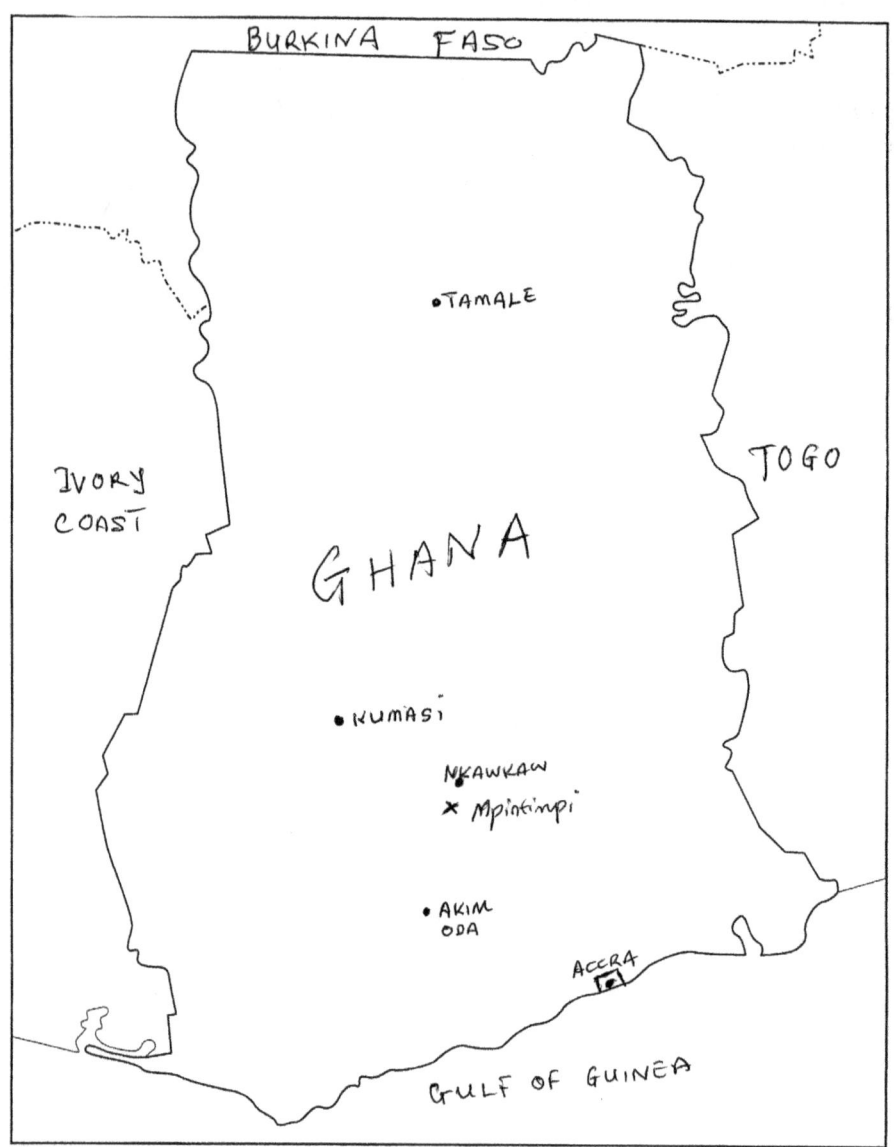

--1--
A TOURIST'S GUIDE TO MPINTIMPI

I GREW UP IN THE SMALL VILLAGE bearing the big name Mpintimpi. The village was indeed so tiny that one of my classmates at primary school used to boast that he was capable of urinating around the whole settlement in one go!

That was my friend Kwadwo Adjei, in his element! A native of Nyafoman, a village about three kilometres to the north of Mpintimpi, where children from the little settlement had to walk to school, he was well known for his bragging. On close contemplation, his claim was after all not so far from the truth, for Mpintimpi indeed was a tiny settlement boasting only a handful of buildings. Because it was such a small place, I think I can afford to take the reader on a quick tour around the village without unduly boring him or her.

Before I do that, I want to mention two points of reference that will recur on several occasions in my narration. These are the two district capitals of the area—Nkawkaw and Akim Oda. Nkawkaw is situated about thirty kilometres to the north of Mpintimpi, while Akim Oda lies about eighty kilometres to the south of the little village.

At that time the main road linking the two towns passed through the heart of the settlement, dividing it into almost two equal halves. This road was not tarred. Today, a new road has been constructed. It no longer passes directly through the village, and runs about fifty metres away from its northern outskirt.

Approaching the village from Nkawkaw, the first building on the left side of the road was our home. A small rectangular mud building measuring about ten metres in length and five metres in breadth, it rose to about three metres above the ground. Like many other buildings in the village, it had a roof made of corrugated aluminium sheets. It boasted two rooms. One room was shared by mother and her three daughters, while the other was reserved for her five boys.

About thirty metres away from the main building, towards the bush that bordered our compound, was a smaller building, about a third the size of the main building. Unlike the bigger building, this second building was covered with sheets woven from the raffia palm. It served as a kitchen and also storage for foodstuffs, firewood and other utensils such as wooden mortar for pounding *fufu*. (More about *fufu* later!) In one corner of the kitchen was a makeshift stove made of clay. Cooking was done with the help of firewood.

There was another stove on the open compound between the two buildings. Much of the cooking, as well as our day-to-day activities, took place in the open space between the two buildings. This was made possible by the generous African weather. When it became too hot, we sought refuge under the shade in the kitchen or under the trees standing on the compound—mango, orange, coconut as well as palm trees.

About ten metres behind the kitchen a makeshift rectangular structure that opened to the tropical weather served as our bathroom. We did not have our own toilet. We shared the communal latrine at the other end of the village with the rest of the community.

With the help of mother, father built the compound for his wife and their children when they got married. He, for his part, continued to reside in his extended family home. Mother left in the evenings to join father in his room. She took along the children who were too young to fend for themselves, whereas the big ones were left behind.

Heading towards the centre of the village, the next building on our side of the road belonged to Maame Gyamfuah. She was several years mother's senior. In the course of time a type of mother–daughter relationship developed between the two women. Whenever mother had problems in her marriage, Maame Gyamfuah was the first person she confided in.

Maame Gyamfuah was married to Papa Kwabena. Papa Kwabena, as in the case of father, did not dwell in the house he had built for his wife and their children, but resided instead in *his* extended family home, situated about fifty metres on the other side of the road. I will devote some lines to Papa Kwabena when I make a stop at his extended family home.

Maame Gyamfuah and Papa Kwabena had several children. One of them was Teacher Acheampong. As his name suggests, he was a teacher by profession, teaching at an elementary school in a little town several miles away from our own. He was a likeable personality, one of the favourites of the village. One day he left his position and returned to the village. Soon news began to spread in the little settlement that he was gravely ill. In due time there was constant coming and going in the house as residents took turns to visit him. I was too young to visit him myself.

Mother returned on her first visit one day, looking very sad indeed.

"What is the matter?" one of us asked.

"I am so concerned for Teacher Acheampong."

"Why?"

"His stomach has swollen up. I think it is full of fluid."

"They should send him to hospital!"

"The extended family members are trying to pool their resources to take him to Nkawkaw. I doubt that he will make it, though. And to think that he is so young, barely thirty years old!"

Mother returned a few days later from one of her regular visits with tears in her eyes.

"Has he passed away?" I wanted to know.

"Not yet; I do not think it will be long, though. Indeed, he has almost given up the fight. His spirits have been dampened by a dream that he had. He told me I was the only person he wanted to confide in."

"What dream?"

"In the dream he told me an elderly woman of his extended family (I won't reveal the name to you) had appeared to him to threaten him and warn him not to go to hospital. Even if he did, it would be of no use for she would go before him to the hospital and neutralise the efforts of the doctors."

You need to know that in that village we lived in a society in which the belief in the power of witchcraft was widespread. The young man had interpreted the dream to mean that the family member involved had already executed him in the spiritual realm. The act was now being manifested in the physical. He passed away a few days after revealing his dream to mother. There was much weeping and wailing for him in the little community.

Next, we move to the compound of Maame Afia, who was also a trusted friend of mother's. Whenever she was in need of foodstuffs or any other basic necessity of life, she approached mother for help; it was not a one-way path, I hasten to add. Mother also approached her to collect whatever she needed.

Directly behind Maame Afia's compound, away from the main road, was the home of Maame Asi Mansa. The women had one thing in common—they were both married to Papa Tawiah, Maame Afia being his first wife. Papa Tawiah was a close relative of Nana (title of Chief) Kofi Poku, Chief of the village. Indeed, he had his bedroom at the palace, which was next to the two homes he had built for his wives.

The compounds of both women were open to each other, allowing the children of both 'rivals' to interact. Not only did the children interact with each other but, owing to the close proximity of their respective homes, the paths of both women crossed on a few occasions during the day. If ever there was tension between the two, they concealed it from the public, for rarely did one witness an open dispute between them.

As already mentioned, the next building from those of the two women was the palace. There resided Nana Kofi Poku, the Chief of the little settlement. The office of a chief in an Akan* setting is not an elected one. The head of the community occupies a special stool, the symbol of power and authority. In each community a specific extended family is custodian of the stool. Only members of that particular extended family have the right of occupancy. It is worthy of note that among the Akans, inheritance is passed along the matrilineal rather than the patrilineal line. In other words, it is not one's children and wife who have a right

---

* Akan people are an ethnic linquistic group in Ghana: their main language is Twi of inheritance, but rather it is one's sisters, brothers, nieces as well as relations from the matrilineal side who possess that right.

Though there are communities in which the palace is by no means the most prominent building, by dint of accident that happened to be the case at Mpintimpi.

Behind the palace, completely blocked from the view of anyone on the main road by the prominent building, was a small building that served as the kitchen for Maame Yaa, the Chief's 'other half'. (It is worthy of note that, contrary to the general trend in the polygamous setting, Nana Kofi Poku had only one wife.)

Next we move to father's extended family home.

Before I continue, however, I will make a small digression to explain the term 'extended family' as understood by us. Elsewhere when one talks about 'family' one usually has in mind the nuclear family involving husband, wife and their children. The net in the 'nuclear' family setting could be slightly spread to include immediate cousins, aunts, nieces, grandparents and grandchildren. That is as far as it usually goes.

Not so the term 'family' in a setting like that of Mpintimpi. Strictly speaking, as far as residents in that area are concerned, there is nothing like a 'nuclear' family. The term 'family' might as well be interchanged with the term 'extended family'. I think one might better speak of the 'extended-extended family', for the family in our setting can indeed be extended. If the half-brother of your great-grandfather was married to the niece of my great-great grandmother, you could still call me your brother or sister as the case may be.

As far as the Akans are concerned, the family line is traced along the matrilineal line. Strictly speaking, my wife and my children are not part of my 'family'. They belong to my *wife's* family. Following the same thinking, it is the children of my sisters and my nieces and aunts along the matrilineal line that are part of my family! Usually each extended family has a home. Usually, when a male member living in the home marries, the wife moves to live with him in his extended family home. To avoid friction, those who can afford it put up extra homes for their wives where they spend the day with their children.

Father's extended family was typical of several other extended family homes in the area. It was a large rectangular building of mud that had a large courtyard in the heart of the building where many of the activities of the inhabitants—cooking, washing, ironing, etc—took place. The building was covered with corrugated aluminium sheets and boasted about eight sleeping rooms. Father occupied what was generally known as a 'hall and chamber'. The 'hall' served as a living room, whereas the 'chamber' was the sleeping room.

Before he left to work on the farm, he came to check on us to make sure everything was alright. On his return from a busy day's work, he rested for a while in his 'hall' before once again coming to us to reassure himself that we were doing fine.

A few years before my eyes saw the light of day, he married a second wife. As expected, his attention was divided between his two wives. This meant he no longer had to call only on us, but on the home of his second wife as well.

Although, whenever his busy schedule in the farm permitted, he would hang around in the homes of his wives and also took some meals there, he insisted on eating the main meal of the day in the home of his extended family.

Unless they were prevented by ill-health and also during the time of their menstrual cycle (a woman was considered 'unclean' during her period and was not permitted to cook for her husband), mother and later my stepmother both cooked for him every day.

Before they had children big enough to assume the role, the women carried the evening meal to their husband. In the course of time when their children were big enough to do so, the duty fell on them to do so. The meal was placed in suitable dishes and packed in a tray. It was customary to cover the dishes with decent looking towels. On his/her arrival, the courier placed the tray on the dining table, or beneath it on occasions when it was already occupied by a meal prepared by his/her stepmother. The meals cooked by his two wives were eaten on a 'first come first served' basis.

When a boy was very young, he ate his meal at the home of his mother. On attaining an age deemed suitable by his father, the junior was invited by the senior to join him at the table. It was a privilege to be invited by your father to eat at his table—it was a sign of the coming of age. At one stage, father extended the invitation to Kwame (two years my senior) and me to join him and our elder brothers at the table. In the course of time the invitation was extended to Kwabena, a few years my junior and the first son of my stepmother, to join us too.

About two hundred metres behind father's family home, along a path that led into the woods, was the communal refuse dump. About twenty metres still further down the road was a rectangular mud building that housed the female latrine that served the whole community.

Next to father's extended family home, was the home of Nana Abenaa Nuro (the term 'Nana' can be used either for a Chief or for one's grandparents), my paternal grandmother. As father used to tell us, our paternal grandfather passed away not long after his birth. Several years later, his mother married Papa Yaw Mensah. The marriage produced twelve children. Father thus boasted several half- brothers and sisters.

Behind that building, away from the main road, was the home of Papa Asante and his family. As I learnt from father, Papa Asante moved to the little village about the time of my birth to cultivate a piece of land he had bought from one of the residents.

A patch of bush, stretching about ten metres along the main road, separated the home of Nana Abenaa Nuro from that of the next compound on that side of the road—the last on that side of the road, as it happened. In it dwelt 'Tailor' and his family. As the name implies, he was a tailor by profession. Tailor and his family were different in one respect—they did not belong to the majority Twi tribe. They were instead Ewes who had moved from their home in the eastern part of the country to dwell in our midst. Like the majority of the inhabitants, however, they were also peasant farmers.

For the reader not conversant with the make-up of the population of Ghana, it is important to know that the population of Ghana is not homogenous, but made up of several tribes that speak entirely different languages from one another. One might think of the relationship between the Japanese, English and Portuguese languages. Hardly any conflict arose on the grounds of one's tribe, however. Indeed, Tailor became one of the most popular citizens in the community.

The last building structure on that side of the road housed the communal male latrine, which was situated about ten metres away from the roadside. That was as far as the village stretched. I would estimate the distance from our home to the other end of the village as approximately 150 metres.

Next, I will take the reader to the other side of the road and continue from there back to the other end of the village.

At the time I was big enough to go to school, there was no school at Mpintimpi. In the course of time, the population of the settlement grew to the point when the authorities recognised the need to start a primary school there. The school was built on the outskirts of the village, on the other side of the road where we are at the moment.

About twenty metres away from the school was the home of Papa Akwasi Kuma. He lived in his big compound with his two wives. He belonged also to the Ewe tribe, having moved to the little village to cultivate the land several years before I was born. Papa Akwasi Kuma happened to be a good friend of father's. Occasionally we went to their home to play. Though they were at home in the Twi language, probably in an effort to get us to learn their language they occasionally gave us instructions in their language. Even today, I still remember the Ewe invitation to join in a meal: *va me dunu*.

At the time I was growing up, there was a large open space between Papa Akwasi Kuma's compound and the next building on that side of the road. When I was about ten years old, rumours began to spread to the effect that the CMB was planning to put up a building in our little village. What does CMB stand for? You may well ask! It stands for Cocoa Marketing Board. Later on in my narration, I will return to have a closer look at cocoa, the main cash crop of Ghana. Then, as now, the CMB, a governmental agency, purchased cocoa beans from the farmers for further processing within the country and export. (The bulk was exported.) Though several other firms have in the meantime sprung up to compete with it, at the time I was growing up the CMB had the lion's share of the market in the country. As far as Mpintimpi was concerned, it was the sole purchaser.

The cocoa farmer at Mpintimpi was in a sense blessed in having a local purchasing agent for cocoa. In several other cocoa-producing areas of the country, residents had to walk distances carrying sacks of cocoa beans on their heads or necks to the next available purchasing agent. Prior to putting up their own building, the local CMB operated from the extended family home of Papa Yaw Mensah. They had rented a hall and an office for this purpose.

Not long after the news began to circulate in the village, we woke up one morning to the deafening sound of heavy earth-moving machinery approaching the village from the direction of Nkawkaw.

At home, we thought they were probably heading for Afosu, the comparatively bigger settlement about five kilometres to the south. But no, on reaching the centre of our village, they made a stop. The mere fact that the huge machines had parked in the village centre was a source of great excitement not only for me, but also for my peers. Clothed only in our *pietos* (children's slips), we soon poured into the street, hopping, jumping, cheering and waving in excitement! We drew as near as the drivers would permit us to have a closer look at the huge metal monsters. I was particularly fascinated by the rolling metal wheels of the caterpillar excavators as well as the huge tyres of the motor graders. Soon the drivers of the construction machines went into action to prepare the piece of land I have already referred to for the construction of the new building to house the CMB.

Over the next several months, economic activity boomed in our little village. Although the construction firm brought some workers with them, they also needed local labour. Eventually several able-bodied men and women, not only from Mpintimpi but also from the surrounding villages, were employed as casual labourers—collecting gravel and sand, mixing concrete, producing concrete blocks, as masons and mason assistants, etc. Several women in the village, including mother, set up 'chop bars' where the construction workers went to 'fill' their stomachs.

After about six months of brisk activity, the large 'cocoa shed', as it came to be known, was complete. It comprised of a huge storage hall, measuring about fifty by twenty metres, where the cocoa beans were kept prior to their transportation to the harbour, and also served as an office for the clerk. Connected to the main building at one end was a smaller building that served as a residence for the clerk. To this day, the cocoa shed remains one of the most prominent buildings in the village.

Three important persons resided in the compound next to the CMB—a compound in which resided other extended family members of Nana Kofi Poku, the village Chief. The first of the three was Nana

Abenaa, the Queen of the little village, the elder sister of the Chief. At the time I was big enough to understand my environment, she was almost blind, and had to be led around the village by one of her grandchildren. Nana Abenaa was a decent and well-respected member of the community.

Then there was Papa Teacher, who was junior both to the Chief and the Queen. As the name implies, he was a teacher by profession, having taught in several places during his long career. He had in the meantime retired and returned to his village to cultivate the land. At that time he pastored the Presbyterian Church, one of two churches in the village.

The third leading personality in the building that was home to several other members of their extended family was Papa Osei. He could, without exaggeration, be referred to as the 'village doctor'. Papa Osei—what a person he was! He never received any formal education. He had neither an idea of human anatomy nor of pathology. Terms like physiology, biochemistry, pharmacology sounded like Latin in his ears. Yet he dutifully and meticulously went about practising his art of healing—from the common cold to severe malaria; from the ordinary headache to migraine; from menstrual pain to the inability of a woman to bear children. Whatever the ailment, he was the first person residents of the village contacted to help cure their condition. In time his name spread far beyond the boundaries of our small village as the sick travelled many kilometres to consult him.

We now arrive at one of the most prominent buildings in the settlement. Two important individuals lived there—Papa Yaw Mensah as well as Papa Kwabena. They were brothers, the former being the elder of the two. As I just indicated, it used to house the local CMB.

As I stated earlier, Papa Yaw Mensah was father's stepfather. He resided in his extended family home with several other members of his traditional African family. After he had had several children with my paternal grandmother, he married a second wife, Maame Tomo. One of the children of Maame Tomo was Moses who became one of my closest associates. He was a brilliant pupil and could also have travelled far on the academic ladder had he also got the chance to move into a secondary school. He could have made it, but he could not find anyone to pay for his boarding fees. In the end he ended up with a middle school leaving certificate, which could not take him very far.

Papa Kwabena, to whom I referred earlier, was married to Maame Gyamfuah, our direct neighbour on the same side of the road. For his orderliness, hard work, discipline and sense of duty, he earned the nickname 'German-Buroni' which, translated, means literally 'the white man from Germany'. He was indeed a hardworking individual who had little patience for those who in his eyes were lazy and unwilling to shed enough sweat to accomplish something in life. He could also be described as a 'no-nonsense' type of person who, for the most part, was not only serious about himself but also about the rest of the world around him.

It was his custom to leave home early in the morning to work on his farm. In the afternoon, one might see him returning from the fields with a heavy load made up of all possible items on his head as well as on both shoulders. One might be forgiven, then, for thinking the daily chores of German-Buroni had ended! But no! After he had rested for a while, he got up, took his machete and headed for the woods yet again! One could only wonder what was driving him to the woods at that time of day.

Was he on his way to inspect the traps he had set for rodents, such as the grasscutter? Was he on his way to the Nwi River to inspect his fish traps? Was he on his way to get some assignment done on another field? Two or three hours later one would find him returning to the village, once again bearing a heavy load. Even then it would be premature to conclude that the daily chores of German-Buroni beyond the borders of his home were over for the day. Again, no! Minutes later he would be seen heading for the woods for the third time—God only knew what for!

The building in which Papa Kwabena resided, together with that of the palace that stood almost directly opposite it on the other side of the road, was a popular meeting place for the children and youth of the village at night—especially on moonlit nights. This was by virtue of the fact that both were located at the very heart of the little settlement.

Sometimes the meetings turned noisy. The majority of the residents in the building were not bothered. (If they were, then at least they did not express it.) Not so Papa Kwabena! He was quick to react at the least opportunity by warning us either to behave ourselves or else quit the premises. Children, children! Often we failed to realise how serious German-Buroni was with his threats and continued to shout and yell on top of our voices! True to his nature, he soon emerged with a long stick he kept purposely for such an occasion to drive away the troublemakers. Woe betide anyone who was not quick enough to seek a safe distance! That person risked receiving a couple of whips to the body.

Even during the latter part of his life, as his eyesight began to fail him, German- Buroni kept a firm hold of his principles. Although he could no longer visit his farms as often as he would want to, the necessary strength to enable him to come out to drive away offending children from his premises never forsook him.

Concealed from the main road by the building just described was the home of Maame Kakraba, father's second wife. As the story goes, after father and mother had been married for about ten years, the parents of a young woman, impressed by his hard work and sense of duty, offered him their daughter in marriage. Father accepted the offer. Mother, as might be expected, was not happy with the new development. As she later told us, she decided to live with the changed situation because she feared her children might be disadvantaged had she decided to leave.

It was not father who built the home for his second wife—it was put up by Papa Kofi Du, her uncle. He lived at Afosu, a town about five kilometres to the south of Mpintimpi, but had a few cocoa farms at Mpintimpi. He entrusted the building to the care of his niece, keeping only a small room that he occupied during his occasional visits to the village.

About one hundred metres away from stepmother's home, somehow isolated from the rest of the village, was the Presbyterian Church. It was built with mud and measured about ten metres in length and five metres in width. Its walls rose to about three metres above the ground. It boasted a roof made of corrugated aluminium sheets. Inside the building were two rows of seven wooden benches. Each bench was capable of seating five worshippers.

Returning to the main road and continuing down the road, we come to the home of Maame Adwoa Nimo. She was a widow, her husband having passed away several years before I was born. One of her children, Atta Kofi, was a good friend of my brothers and I. On several occasions he joined us on one of our regular expeditions to hunt for Gambian pouched rats and grasscutters (more on that topic later).

The next building along the road was erected by Papa Osei, the 'village doctor', for his wife. As I learnt from mother, Papa Osei used to be addicted to alcohol. For a while he appeared more interested in satisfying his cravings for alcohol than the need to settle down to marry and raise a family. One day he returned from one of his journeys through the surrounding villages to inform his family members that he had overcome his addiction.

"That is a joke!" one of them remarked.

"No, it isn't", Papa Osei said, and added "The Lord Jesus Christ has set me free!"

"You must indeed be losing your mind from too much drinking!" another retorted.

"No, I am not!" he insisted. "Someone I met on one of my journeys took me to his church. After the service I accepted Christ into my life. Now I am free."

Initially hardly any of them thought he could give up his drinking habit. He had on several previous occasions failed in his attempts to do so, and so they had all given up hope that he could ever succeed in turning away from drink.

This time, however, he did indeed overcome his addiction for ever. In the end, he opened a branch of the Apostolic Church, the church in which he gave his life to Jesus. The Church held its worship services in a large room in the home he had built for his young and attractive wife who was also a member of the Apostolic Church.

The next building belonged to the extended family of Maame Adwoa Adeye and her brother Papa Ankoma. They were our direct neighbours just across the main road. Partly as a result of that a close bond of friendship developed between the inhabitants of both compounds. Later in this narration, I will talk about a very special relationship that developed between two individuals, one from each of the two homes.

At the time I was growing up, the compound of Maame Adwoa Adeye happened also to be the first one on that side of the road approaching the village from Nkawkaw. In the course of time, Kofi Dagarti, who arrived from the north of the country to look for work as a casual labourer on the fields of the cocoa farmers, erected a small building to house himself and his wife, Adwoa Dagarti.

Later Papa Kwasi Bruku, who became a good friend of father's, also arrived to cultivate a piece of land he had acquired from one of the inhabitants. He built his house behind that of Maame Adwoa Adeye, away from the main road.

Several metres behind the property of Papa Bruku was the football field constructed through the sweat of the local football team. I will return to the football pitch later in my story.

That ends the tour around my little village. Thank you, dear reader, for bearing with me.

Someone may want to know the population of the village at that point in time. The answer is that there was no official figure for that. My guess is that it was around one hundred.

--2--
THE ARDUOUS JOURNEY OF THE NEW ARRIVAL TO OUR HOME

AS WAS THE CASE with almost every child who was born in Mpintimpi, my birth took place at home. According to mother, a small rectangular wooden structure that served as the family bathroom was my 'labour ward'. It measured about one metre in length and eighty centimetres in width. The wooden wall rose to about a metre and a half above ground level. At the top, the structure was open to the free tropical skies. The floor was not cemented but covered with fine gravel. As in the case of many of the births that took place in the village, Papa Osei, the 'village doctor', was the main person in charge of affairs. He was helped by a few elderly women of the settlement.

By the time I was big enough to understand my environment, there were seven children at home—five boys and two girls. I had four elder brothers and two younger sisters. In the course of time I noticed that mother's stomach was growing bigger and bigger with the days. Soon the news made the rounds that a new arrival was expected in our home.

Then one day mother disappeared into the family bathroom. Prior to doing so, she sent one of us on an errand to fetch Maame Gyamfuah and Maame Adwoa Adeye. Not long thereafter the two women rushed into our compound.

"Where is your mother?" they asked, as if with one voice. We pointed to the bathroom. Soon both women rushed in there. For the next several hours they remained with mother in the small enclosure. After a while, one of them emerged. We could read the anguish in her eyes. Turning to one of my senior brothers, she began:

"Hurry up and fetch Papa Osei. Tell him we need his help urgently."

Not long thereafter, Papa Osei came rushing to our home and joined the women. I was too young to understand what exactly was going on. The expression on the faces of the adults led me, however, to believe that all was not well with her.

Finally, about an hour after the arrival of the 'village doctor', we could hear the screams of a baby. It was followed almost immediately by the claps and shouts of joy of the three adults attending to mother. Several minutes later, mother, who seemed to be in terrible pain, emerged, assisted by the two women. Tenderly, they led her into her bedroom. She remained there for the rest of the day.

Poverty, deprivation, destitution, want—you can go on listing all the epithets or words we associate with a state of impoverishment—were my best companions as I was growing up in little Mpintimpi.

Though several years have passed since then, I still remember that when I was very young, I possessed a disproportionately big head and stomach. As a result of that, whenever I walked around the little settlement clothed only with a *pieto*, I was taunted not only by my peers, but also by some of the adults with calls of "bin tom, tom!" (referring to my protruding belly) and coconut head.

I was highly tempered as a child, I can tell you! Needless to say, I was easily infuriated by their taunts. In my anger, I got hold of a small stone (they abounded on the streets of the little village) and threatened to throw it at the offender. Whether I did indeed on occasion carry out my threat is something I can no longer recall.

I just could not understand why anyone would be so mean to me! Concerning my alleged big head, I really do not think it was all that big! Even if it really was, it gained extra prominence because, I think, I was too small for my age, a situation that, without doubt, would have arisen from malnutrition.

In regard to my stomach, it might well be due to *kwashiorkor*! As I have since learnt, *kwashiorkor*, a local Ghanaian term that has gained international usage, is a condition found in children with a chronic deficiency of protein in their diet. *Kwashiorkor* might not have been the sole cause of my problem, however! Parasitic worms were a widespread condition not only at Mpintimpi but in several parts of the country. That should come as no surprise considering the prevalent hygienic conditions.

Even as I write, I remember an occasion when my parents, suspecting that worms might be the cause of my distended stomach, gave me to drink *nsonsonaduro*, literally 'worm medicine', they had bought from the weekly market at Nyafoman. Even today, I remember the pleasant taste of the green-looking 'worm medicine'.

To verify their suspicion, mother did not leave me to empty my bowels in the public latrine. Instead, she gave me a chamber pot for that purpose. This is no exaggeration but the bare truth, dear reader. The worms that came out of my bowels! They were not tiny bits, but rather long round worms, about 30cm long and about 5mm in diameter. There were *loads* of them, coiled together in a large bundle! They looked like the large earthworms I saw on my way to our various farms or the riverside. Indeed, they looked very alike.

Today, I know they carry the medical term *Ascaris lumbricoides* or *Roundworms*, which, of course, are quite different from earthworms. That they made their home in my bowels and competed with me for the very food my parents managed to put on the table was a display of unbelievable impudence on their part!

--3--
RECRUITING FOR THE ACADEMIC JOURNEY

ON 6TH MARCH 1957, Ghana, then the Gold Coast, gained independence from the British. The first post-independence administration, headed by Dr Kwame Nkrumah, the man who led the country into independence, soon introduced free and compulsory education for all. The policy of compulsory education was enforced to the very letter. Aware that some among the farming population who hitherto had relied on the helping hands of their children would be reluctant to send them to school, the Government sent school inspectors around to enforce the rule. Woe betide the parent who tried to prevent their children from attending school!

It was during that time I was sent to school. How could the authorities determine that any child had reached school-going age? The overwhelming majority of us did not possess birth certificates—if indeed any of us had that important document at all!

Several years have elapsed since then but I still remember how the 'recruitment' exercise was carried out in our little village. With our pieces of cotton clothes, *ntama*, wrapped around our bodies, we assembled on the veranda in front of the palace. One after the other, each of us was asked to use one arm to make a bow over the head and attempt to touch the ear on the other side of his/her body. Whoever was able to do so was deemed mature enough to begin the academic journey.

It was customary for children about to start school to adopt a 'Christian name'. Neither myself nor my older brother, Kwame, who was also about to start school, boasted 'Christian names'. Father and mother, both illiterate, had no idea of such names. The task eventually fell on Ransford, who had gone quite far in his education to help his two junior brothers out on the matter. His method was not without ingenuity. First, he wrote down several European first names familiar to his. Next, he instructed us to listen attentively as he read them out. The rule was for us to shout "STOP!" should he call out a name that appealed to us. We don't quite remember any longer as to which of the two of us first asked Ransford to stop at a name. In any case, Kwame was so excited by the sound of the name 'Edmund' that he responded at once. For my part I plumped for Robert.

We had to wear a uniform. For the boys it was khaki shirts and khaki trousers. This applied to every boy attending the state schools. As far as the girls were concerned, the colour of their uniform could be green, blue, pink or white, depending on the choice of the school concerned.

As we left home for school for the very first time, hardly any of the pupils heading from Mpintimpi to attend the school at Nyafoman wore the prescribed uniform. Instead, we were clothed in our traditional *ntama*, which we usually wrapped loosely around our body. To prevent the article of clothing from slipping away from our bodies as we went through the various activities of the school day, we wrapped them in such a way as to permit us to tie two ends loosely around our necks. For a while our teachers tolerated those who attended school without a uniform. A time came, though, when such pupils were sent home and not permitted to return until they had acquired their respective uniforms.

After wearing the same uniform—hardly any parent could afford two sets at a time—for a year or two, it invariably began to show signs of wear and tear. Eventually the small tears developed into real 'potholes'. The time came when the uniform began to reveal almost entirely the clothes being worn beneath it. At the beginning, our teachers would ask us to remind our parents politely about the need to replace them.

"Let's wait for the cocoa harvesting season", they would reply. Sometimes the season passed without any sign of the 'poor uniform' being relieved of its duty. Finally a time came when the class teachers could bear the situation no longer and sent the pupil home to acquire a new uniform.

At the time I began my academic journey the school system in Ghana was made up in the main of three cycles. The first cycle or elementary school took a minimum of six years and a maximum of ten years to complete. From there one could move on to the second cycle or secondary school.

Elementary schools were spread throughout the country. The situation was different in regard to secondary schools. They were found mainly in large towns and cities and were run mostly as boarding schools. Tuition was free in all schools; students who attended the boarding schools were, however, expected to pay for their board and lodging.

Five years of secondary school education ended with the GCE 'O' Level (General Certificate of Education, Ordinary Level) examinations. Those who performed well could proceed to do a two-year sixth form and sit for the GCE 'A' Level (Advanced Level) examinations. Three passes at the 'A' Level was normally required to open the way for admission into university.

For most of the children waking up early at Mpintimpi to prepare for school, the best hope the school system offered was the completion of the ten-year elementary education and the sitting of the final 'Standard Seven' examination, also generally known as 'Hall'. One could then proceed to learn a trade or else find a job as an office clerk, a store assistant, a primary school teacher, etc.

--4--
THE TEDIOUS WALK TO AND FROM SCHOOL

We got up early on a typical school day. The first task for the day was to walk to the Nwi River, about a mile away to fetch water for the home. The water was collected in plastic or aluminium buckets of various sizes, each capable of holding between five to ten litres of water. We carried the load on our heads. On a typical day we undertook two to three trips. In the rainy season, when there was usually sufficient supply of water at home, we were spared that daily early morning routine.

When time permitted, we did have a proper bath; if, on the other hand, we were hard-pressed for time, we washed only our heads, our armpits and both legs from the knee downwards. Next, we hastily ate our breakfast, made up mainly of boiled plantains (a banana-type fruit) and stew.

It was customary for all children from Mpintimpi heading for school at Nyafoman to do so in a single group. The practice was for those who got ready first to go round the homes of the other children to urge them to hurry up. There were times, though, when the group could not wait forever for others to be ready before heading for school.

Children as young as six years old, walking a distance of two miles to school—the mind boggles! And yet that was precisely the case. The bigger ones, those in the upper classes, kept an eye on the little ones as we journeyed on. We walked along the main road leading to Nkawkaw. Though traffic on it was sparse, we could still reckon with a few vehicles passing by in either direction as we walked. The road was not tarred;

beside that, it had potholes in several places. As a result, the vehicles could not travel with any great speed. This allowed us sufficient time to 'park' ourselves along the fringes of the road long before the vehicles reached us.

In the dry season, the passing vehicles left considerable dust in their trails. That was a source of considerable irritation, not only because we were forced to inhale the dust but also because it resulted in our uniforms getting dirty.

If the dust was a source of vexation, then the other factor in the equation, namely the rain, was less comforting. In the geographical region where we lived, it either rained or shined. If it poured down heavily in the morning long before we set out for school, we stayed away from school for that entire day. Usually, however, the rains did not come down early in the morning. Instead, it caught us by surprise just as we were heading for school, or returning home from school. In such situations, we were left with no other choice than to take an involuntary shower, for hardly any of us carried an umbrella. If by chance one of us was carrying a small machete to be used to weed on his or her plot (more on the issue of plots later), we cut the broad leaves of a banana or plantain tree growing in the farms bordering the road and used them as improvised umbrellas.

Sometimes the problems brought by the rain were compounded by the passing vehicles! As I just pointed out, the road was not devoid of potholes. When it rained 'ponds' of water gathered in several places on the road so when the passing vehicles drove through them, they sent splashes of dirty water in all directions to soil our clothes. Some of the drivers left the impression on our minds that they just wanted to show the 'young academics' on the road who really was in charge of the roads, for they drove through 'pothole ponds' that we were sure could have been avoided!

Even if the vehicle passing by on a rainy day did not cause us problems, the mud caused by the rain did so by soiling our feet. Fortunately, there was a small stream a few hundred metres away from school so we headed there and cleaned our feet before reaching the school compound.

The fact that all of us, without exception, walked barefoot to school brought its own peculiar problems. In the dry season, the scorching tropical sun heated the ground we were walking on. As we walked along, we could feel the burning sensation under our soles.

On some occasions, the driver of a vehicle pulled over and gave us a lift! Those were very rare instances, though. In the first place, most of the vehicles that passed by were already filled to the last seat. Even if a vehicle boasted a few unoccupied seats, the fact that we usually walked in a group of not less than six pupils at a time might have dissuaded the driver from pulling to a stop and taking only a fraction along. It is not hard to imagine the consternation on the faces of those who were left behind!

--5--
FLIES AND BEES DISTURBING THE MORNING ASSEMBLY

WE REALLY HAD TO HURRY UP to avoid being late for school, for failure to arrive on time could have serious consequences. Later on, I will look more closely at the forms of punishment meted out to us!

One had to be at school several minutes before the beginning of lessons. Why the need to do so? The task of tidying up the school, the classrooms, the immediate as well as surrounding compound, fell to the schoolchildren.

The whole school population was divided into four sections, named respectively after the colours blue, green, red and yellow. Each section had a leader selected from a pupil in the most senior class; in the case of the primary school this was primary class 6. The section leader in his turn was accountable to the teacher assigned to the section.

The immediate compound surrounding the school was divided among the four sections. The section in turn allotted a piece of plot to each pupil. It was the duty of each pupil to keep his or her portion of plot tidy, including weeding it and also collecting any trash that might have been discarded on it. It was expected of every pupil to visit his or her plot every day to make sure it was tidy. On regular intervals the section teacher or sometimes the head teacher himself, went round to inspect the plots. Such inspections were mostly unannounced! Each pupil had to stand on his or her plot during the inspection. Woe betide anyone whose plot was untidy—he or she risked being caned!

The actual school day began at 8:30 am with an assembly that was held in the open, in front of the school building. Each class lined up in two parallel lines facing the school building, short girls in the very front followed by the tall ones; then the short boys like myself, and finally the tall ones at the rear. Even the manner in which we formed the lines could bring a pupil into trouble. The lines were expected to be straight, and anyone caught disrupting it could be called forward and caned before the whole school. To achieve a decent straight line each of us stretched the right arm and touched the shoulder of the child in front of him or her. After the school prefect or the pupil on duty that day had convinced him or herself that a decent straight line had been formed, the order came for us to put our hands down.

The assembly was opened with a Christian-based meditation. Though it was a state school, that fact did not cause offence to anyone. The population of the area was mostly Christian, the remaining being adherents of various traditional African forms of worship. At that period about twenty per cent of the population of Ghana were Muslims, most of whom lived in Northern Ghana, which was several miles away from the borders of our little village.

The meditation was followed by the recitation of the national pledge. Every pupil had to stand in the 'salute position' during the recitation.

Next, we sang the first stanza of the national anthem. Each one of us was required to stand in the 'attention' position during the singing of the anthem. In our part of the world, it was not unusual on such an occasion for one to be disturbed by a fly or a bee, or both. Still, we were required to be motionless throughout the duration of the singing of the anthem. Those who were caught moving could reckon with a few lashes immediately after the song was over. After we had pledged ourselves to our nation and sung the national anthem, the teacher on duty, or the head teacher, as the case may be, read out the announcements.

Finally, we marched into our classrooms.

The school day was divided into two main sessions, namely the morning and the afternoon. For the primary school, which could be described as Years 1 to 6 of the elementary school, the morning session began at 8:30 am and ended at 11:30 am. This was followed by a lunch break which lasted till 1.30 pm. The afternoon session ended at 3.30 pm.

In the case of the middle school (Year 7 to Year 10) the morning session was from 8:30 am to 12:00 noon followed by a lunch break, which lasted till 1:30 pm. In their case, the afternoon session ended at 4:00 pm.

In the primary school one particular exercise became almost part and parcel of the morning school life. This was commonly known as 'mental'. During 'mental' we were given problems in arithmetic, usually ten, sometimes twenty, calculations to solve mentally. The teacher usually found the time to mark it soon after it was over. One or two errors by a pupil were usually permitted. More errors could result in the pupil being caned.

During the lunch break, our classmates who hailed from Nyafoman returned home to enjoy hot meals prepared by their parents or relatives or, in some cases, by themselves.

Pupils from Mpintimpi and elsewhere who did not call Nyafoman their home had two options as far as the afternoon meal was concerned—either to bring cooked meals along in the morning to be eaten during the break, or to carry raw foodstuffs along that they could cook during the break time.

The second option was favoured by those who happened to have relations or friends who were prepared to allow them into their homes to prepare their meals there. Understandably most of us preferred the second option because of the hot meal it guaranteed. In our case mother had a friend who allowed us to cook our lunch in her home. Other classmates from Mpintimpi and elsewhere who did not enjoy that privilege had to content themselves with eating meals they had carried along in the morning; needless to say, their food had turned cold by the time it was eaten.

If mental arithmetic was a regular exercise for our young brains in the morning, dictation served to achieve a similar purpose during the afternoon session. The teacher read out ten to twenty words that had to be spelt correctly. As in the case of 'mental', those who scored below the accepted mark set by the teacher could be caned.

--6--
THE YOUNG ACADEMIC ON THE POINT OF EXPLOSION

WALKING HOME FROM SCHOOL in the evening was a more tedious undertaking compared to the morning walk to school. Not only was one exhausted from the day's activities, but usually also hungry and thirsty.

Those who might have thought we would enjoy immediate respite on returning home from a tedious day's activity at school will have jumped to a premature conclusion. Indeed, most of our parents took the assistance we would offer them on our return from school into consideration when they set out to prepare our evening meals. As I will later explain in some detail, fufu, our main evening meal, was prepared through a laborious manner of pounding the ingredients in a wooden mortar into balls. The balls are then swallowed down with soup.

Our parents reckoned with our help in pounding fufu on our return from school. Thus they timed their preparation of the favourite meal in such a way as to allow the pounding phase to coincide with our return. One could read the anguish in our faces on returning home from a tedious day at school only to be called upon to pound fufu! Do not blame our parents! They themselves would until then also have endured several hours of bone-breaking work under the tropical heat, both on the farm and at home. The pounding of fufu can take anywhere between half an hour and an hour of laborious work, not devoid of considerable sweating during the process!

Those who have lived in the tropics will bear me out that there is a rapid transition from daylight to darkness. By 7 pm at the latest our little settlement was engulfed in thick darkness. The school day was not over, though. We still needed to do our homework. Our schoolteachers did not reserve homework only for the weekend; they also assigned us with tasks that needed to be resolved overnight, ready to be presented in class the next day.

We did not have access to electricity. Instead, we had to resort to kerosene lanterns or Swiss kerosene lamps and endure the hot blasts of heat that emanated from them! It was no fun learning with those lamps or lanterns. The smell of the burning fuel was, to put it mildly, irritating. While the 'young academic' was already struggling with an assignment, the smell of the burning fuel added salt to the injury. Under such circumstances, any perceived provocation from one or other resident of the home—laughter, a scream, or a shout—could cause the aspiring academic to almost explode with fury.

Finally, at about 9 pm, we retired to bed. "Good night and sleep well!" one would want to wish us. That was indeed well deserved! If only the ubiquitous mosquitoes would understand that! But no! Instead, they came to pester us! One could somehow understand them, for it was our blood that provided them *their* dinner. Whatever trouble the mosquitoes caused, initially, we were so exhausted from the day's activities that they could not prevent sleep from soon overcoming us. The situation changed in the middle of the night, after we had passed through the deep phase of sleep. Soon, one began not only to feel the burning sensation resulting from their bites, but to be terribly irritated by the whistling noise emanating not only from Mr and Mrs Mosquito but also their accompanying offspring!

--7--
THE AWFUL EXPERIENCE WITH THE RED-HOT IRON

WE TRIED TO WASH OUR SCHOOL UNIFORMS on returning home from the farm on Saturdays. When we failed to do so, we performed this chore on Sundays. During the dry season, when water was difficult to come by at home, we carried our dirty items to the Nwi River to get them washed there. During the rainy season, when there was a regular supply of rainwater to fill our water-collecting containers, we did the washing at home. One other reason we avoided the Nwi River at that time of year was because it usually flooded its banks. After washing our clothes with our hands, we left them hanging in the sun to dry.

At this stage, I would like to introduce the reader to the concept of 'starching' our school uniform. The cassava or manioc tuber that abounds in our area is rich in starch. We obtained the starch by scratching the tuber free of its skin against a rough metal surface, adding water to the mixture and finally pouring it on a sieve. The solution so obtained was rich in starch.

There were two ways of applying the starch to our uniform. In the first instance we dipped the uniform into the cold solution and allowed it to dry before pressing it with a charcoal iron. The second method involved first boiling the starch and spraying it on the surface of the uniform, pressing it immediately thereafter.

He or she who wore a decently 'starched' and pressed school uniform to school felt proud of his/her outfit. The matter did not end there; one could win points for his or her section. The converse was also true. One could be penalised with negative points for one's section if one appeared with a school uniform that was either not properly ironed or not ironed at all. In the latter instance one could even be caned for putting on such a uniform to school.

Our parents were so busy performing the daily chores of life that they had practically no time left to help us with the ironing of our school uniform. In the end we were left with no option than to do so ourselves. Sometimes, the elder siblings helped their younger ones perform the task. That was not always the case, however. Sometimes the older siblings felt disrespected by their naughty junior ones and left them to sort out their own affairs.

We rarely pressed our uniforms on tables. Instead, we did so on bed sheets spread on the bare cemented floor of our room. We had to assume the kneeling position beside the sheet to be able to do so. I still remember an awful experience I had one day as I was pressing my school uniform. I was barely ten years old at the time. As I knelt beside the bed sheet spread on the floor, moving the red hot iron to and fro on the uniform, the hotly heated iron tilted in one direction. In the process, I lost my balance. Before I could prevent it, the top part of my right thigh, not far from the organ of urination, came into direct contact with the hot metal!

Even as I write, the screaming and yelling at the top of my voice that resulted is still fresh in my memory. The metal burnt away a chunk of skin, the shape of a triangle measuring about five centimetres at the base and narrowing to about four centimetres on each side. Did I receive any painkillers to soothe the pain? Negative! What about antibiotics to prevent infection? Still negative!

A Twi saying has it that God drives away the ants from the animal deprived of a tail. My parents, in line with that thinking, might have trusted Divine grace to help sort the matter out. And so it happened, for the wound healed without any complications.

--8--
THE CALL TO DISCIPLINE AND THE NEED TO IMPROVISE

AS IN SEVERAL ASPECTS OF LIFE IN THE LITTLE VILLAGE, we had to learn to improvise. Although the Government of the day provided us with free textbooks as well as exercise books, in some areas, as in the case of learning aids, for example, we had to improvise.

One area was counters. Although we could probably have purchased them in the big towns, our teachers, desirous of sparing our parents the extra financial burden, asked us to settle on counters we produced either on our own or with the help of our parents. As counters, we cut branches of some of the trees growing in our area and hewed out fifty or a hundred pieces, as the case may be. These we tied together with plastic or cotton threads. Alternatively, we resorted to beads growing in the area. Each of us collected fifty or a hundred, dividing them into small sacks, and took them along to the arithmetic class.

Each pupil was expected to display a high standard of discipline or else risk being punished. Punishment was usually in the form of lashes to the palm or the buttocks. Our female counterparts, however, were usually spared being caned on the buttocks. Instead, they normally received their lashes upon their palms. The boys on our part could either be lashed on our palms or on our buttocks. One could be caned for various reasons, including the following:

- Failure to keep to the personal standards of hygiene expected of each pupil—keeping fingernails cut, keeping teeth clean,

keeping hair short and combed, keeping school uniform tidy and decently pressed.
- Failure to keep the plot assigned to him/her tidy.
- Failure to get homework done in proper time.
- Failure to score well in mental arithmetic or dictation.
- Chatting in the class in the presence or absence of the class teacher.

Yes, we were expected to be silent even when our class teachers were not around. The responsibility fell on the class captain, sometimes selected solely by the class teacher, sometimes elected by the whole class through secret ballot, to ensure that order was maintained in the class. Failure on his/her part to do so could lead to him/her being punished. To prevent that kind of situation, he/she usually wrote down the names of those who disturbed the silence during the absence of the teacher, to be submitted when called upon to do so. Punishment was not always corporal. The offending pupil could, for example, be called upon to write several lines, sometimes up to five hundred or even more of a sentence, such as

I WILL ALWAYS BE PUNCTUAL FOR CLASS
I WILL NO LONGER DISTURB THE CLASS
I WON'T BE RUDE TO MY TEACHER, etc.

One could also be assigned a portion of the compound to weed, and so forth!

--9--
CALL IT CHILD LABOUR IF YOU WILL!

DURING OUR SCHOOL DAYS, our teachers used us to perform several kinds of jobs. The jobs varied, depending on whether it involved primary or middle school pupils. We could, for example, be used to help a farmer harvest maize. There were two aspects of this. It could be that the farmer had done the harvesting on his own. Our duty was to carry the harvested maize in baskets back home. On certain occasions we did the harvesting as well as transported the produce to the home of the farmer involved.

Rarely could a farmer provide enough baskets for every child. Usually an announcement was made on the day prior to carrying out the job, calling on every pupil to carry a basket or a tray to school. The very young among us, especially those in primary years 1 to 3, were usually exempt from that type of work. If such a job needed to be done, it was usually carried out during the afternoon session; the morning session, on the other hand, was rarely used for non-academic activity.

Later, I will talk in some detail of the making of palm kernel oil in the village. Palm kernel oil is obtained from the kernel, which is embedded in the nut of the fruit of the oil palm. The nut needs to be cracked to obtain the kernel embedded in it. Sometimes, schoolchildren were used to perform that function.

It was not uncommon for the schoolchildren to be called upon to fetch water to fill the water containers of their teachers—or the wives and in some cases the concubines of their teachers! As might be expected, that job was performed mostly in the dry season. We usually collected the water either from wells or the Nwi River, which served Nyafoman also.

One particular job we did was not devoid of danger, namely the cutting of bamboo sticks. The sticks grew widely in the woods around Nyafoman. The bamboo sticks were used in various ways—to build fences or hedges around the school garden to prevent sheep and goats from destroying the crops, or for constructing raised structures to dry cocoa beans, in buildings, etc.

Due to the hazards associated with the cutting, we were usually accompanied by part of the teaching staff who selected those they considered mature enough for the assignment to do the cutting. Other children were left with the duty of carrying the sticks on their heads over a distance of about a mile or more back to school.

Because the bamboo stick could attain considerable heights, it could hardly be carried by a single pupil. Instead, two pupils, one at the head, the other at the tail, were made to carry a single stick back to school.

One may want to know what kind of hazard was posed by the bamboo sticks that we cut. The main one involved the cutting itself. We did so with the help of cutlasses. Sometimes, after one had cut through about half of the stem, it broke with such force that the stick forcefully sprang into the air. In such a situation, one stood in danger of being pierced in the foot, leg or even the body! Though I did not personally witness any of us getting injured on such assignments, reports of cases of schoolchildren elsewhere getting hurt, in some cases seriously, by bamboo sticks made their rounds from time to time.

What happened to the money earned by the school carrying on such activities? Well, our teachers kept reminding us that the money earned was meant for the good of the school—to be used for the purchase of footballs and jerseys for the school team, the acquisition of medication and other material for the first-aid box, and also contributed towards the end of year school feast.

Still, rumours to the effect that our teachers 'chopped' (a local terminology that stands for embezzled) our money did not cease to circulate! One wild rumour had it that during one staff meeting a furious exchange ensued between one member of staff and the head teacher, the junior accusing his superior of embezzling school funds. Tempers were said to have flared to the point that blows were exchanged!

--10--
THE SCHOOL FEAST AND THE DAY OF RECKONING

"**OUR DAY**" WAS A SCHOOL FEAST to mark the end of a term. The common practice was for each class to organise a feast to mark the end of the first and second terms. The feast for the end of the third term, the end of the academic year, usually involved the whole school.

When the feast was organised by a class, the teacher asked pupils to bring their share of food from home. One had the option to enjoy it alone or share it with friends. The latter was usually the case. Usually friends joined their tables together and enjoyed their meals together, eating from the same dish. It was an advantage on such occasions to have friends whose parents were well-to-do, who could afford to prepare rich meals that one's own parents could not afford.

At the end of the school year, many schools invested part of the money earned during the academic year performing various jobs to throw a party for the whole school population. Depending on how much money the school could afford, a sheep or a goat or several fowl were acquired for the purpose. Usually rice and yams went with a tasty sauce.

Before we were dismissed home for each holiday, our teachers handed out our terminal reports. This was not done confidentially, on an individual basis, but rather before the whole class. That was the case at the end of the first and second terms. At the end of the third term, the ritual took place before an assembly of the whole school.

Whatever the setting, the ritual followed a similar pattern. The class teacher stood in front of the class or the school and, beginning from the pupil who attained the overall best mark in all the subjects downwards, he/she called out the names of the class. At the call of each name, the pupil concerned stepped forward to collect his/her terminal report. The accompanying applause grew less intense until it ceased altogether by the time it was the turn of the fifth or sixth pupil.

One might imagine the expression on the faces of fellow classmates, as name after name followed and they failed to hear their names! The tension was particularly high during the end of year gathering, when a pupil might realise for the first time that he/she would have to repeat the class. When the news finally came home to such pupils, some of them broke down in tears; for a while some were inconsolable. It was a pathetic sight to behold.

--11--
MY COUSIN THE DRIVER

OUR PARENTS could not afford to provide us with toys, so we improvised our own. Among other things we built our own cars. My cousin, Kwaku Driver, had a particular obsession with building cars. It was indeed his obsession with anything that moved on four wheels that earned him the nickname 'Driver'.

Kwaku designed and constructed his own toy cars making use of the fibre from the branches of the raffia palm. Whether it was a Bedford truck, a Mercedes Benz bus, or a Toyota pick-up, my cousin was capable of building toy imitations of almost every model of a vehicle known to him.

With the help of the raffia palm, after we built the body of the vehicle, we were left with the tyres to fit on our vehicles. For this the root of the Onyina tree provided the answer. Onyina is a tree that grows in our part of the world. These trees can attain considerable sizes and also heights. The roots of the young tree were particularly suited for the purpose, being evenly round in circumference. Besides that, it is not particularly hard, which enabled us to cut a wheel out of it using our machetes.

To obtain the roots, we selected a suitable tree and traced one or more of the roots, which can grow several metres from the stem, towards the periphery. We then dug around it to lay it bare of soil. Finally we severed it from the main stem and carried it home. Back home we cut appropriate sizes of the root into tyres, which we fitted to our brand new 'vehicles'.

--12--
THE VILLAGE NEWS BROADCASTER AND THE NAUGHTY CHILDREN

THE OFFICE OF THE 'GONG-GONG BEATER' at Mpintimpi can be likened to that of the press spokesperson at the White House in Washington, at 10 Downing Street in London, or the Bundeskanzleramt in Berlin. (In some ways he is like the town crier of olden times in Britain, who rang a bell before making public announcements on the streets.)

Selected by the Chief from one of the young men of the community, this personage had the duty of announcing to the community any important news or event they needed to know about. This could be something the Chief himself wanted to pass on to his subjects, or an event or happening that someone living there wished to pass on to the wider community.

Such an individual cannot on his or her own request the gong-gong beater to spread the news item on his or her behalf. Instead, tradition requires that he/she calls first on the Chief to inform him about the matter. The head of the community in turn authorises the gong-gong beater to spread the news to the community as a whole.

How does the gong-gong beater go about his job in Mpintimpi? He does so along the main road, that, as I mentioned earlier, divides the little settlement into two almost equal halves. Beginning from one end of the road, he moves along the road towards the other end spreading his message. *Kon-kon; kon-kon; kon-kon,* he beats hard on his gong. "*M-p-*

i-n-t-i-m-p-i-fo-e!!" he screams at the top of his voice. "I extend warm greetings from Nana. He has asked me to pass such-and-such messages on to you!" *Kon-kon; kon-kon*—he beats his gong again to signify the end of the announcement. He then moves on. After a distance of about fifty metres he stops, beats his gong once again and repeats the message. From there he walks another fifty or so metres and repeats the ritual. And so, on and on he goes, moving along the streets of the settlement, beating his gong and broadcasting the message of the Chief to the ears of everyone in every corner of the community.

It was one of the favourite pastimes of my peers and I to follow the gong beater as he went about his duty. Children, children! On some occasions, we did not keep silent as we did so, but instead yelled and cried out at the top of our voices, repeating what he had just announced to the community. The community announcer would then turn to us and plead with us to behave decently. For a short while, we obeyed him and comported ourselves in an orderly fashion. Soon, however, one or more of us began to shout at the top of his/her voice. At that stage he would turn to chase us away. Whoever was first to be caught could expect a knock on the head, even though he/she might be innocent.

The gong-gong beater was not paid for his job. However, to compensate him for his role, society exempted him from direct participation in communal labour.

--13--
JOINING FORCES FOR THE COMMON GOOD

THE COMMUNITY CAME TOGETHER on a regular basis to perform assignments beneficial to the community as a whole. Such activities came to be known as communal labour. They were not unique to our little settlement but were practised in several parts of the country. Usually the community set aside a particular day of the week during which they would meet for that purpose. In the case of Mpintimpi, it was Wednesday.

How often the society met for communal labour was not laid down. Instead, it depended on the specific need of the society. There were occasions when weeks, even months, passed without the need for the Chief to call the residents together to work for the common good of the society. On other occasions, for example when a new latrine or a new school block had to be constructed, the community met every Wednesday over the next several weeks to carry out the specific project.

Other occasions that called for the coming together of the whole community was the need to weed around the fringes, or periphery of the village, clear the path that led to the Nwi River of the weeds that threatened to encroach it, and weeding around the male and female latrines, etc.

It was customary for the gong-gong beater to go round the settlement on the evening prior to such a meeting to announce the event. This was done, even if everyone was aware of the day, so as to prevent those who failed to show up excusing themselves of having forgotten about it.

Usually communal labour was performed separately by the sexes. Occasionally, however, a joint session, involving both sexes was held. This was particularly the case when a new building project was undertaken, notably for the school. In that case, the women were sent to fetch the water needed for the project from the Nwi River.

Every adult who was not prevented by reason of ill health was expected to take part in the day's activities. Only the Chief and the gong-gong beater were exempt. Even though not expected to do so, the Chief usually was present, and appeared to serve as a morale-booster for his subjects. Failure to take part in communal labour without a convincing excuse could lead to the imposition of a fine by the Town Development Committee. This could be in the form of money, a pot of palm wine, a bottle of akpeteshie, or a combination of any of the three.

--14--
THE TREACHERY OF THE FARMER'S KIDS EXPOSED

THEN, AS NOW, THE RESIDENTS OF MPINTIMPI engaged in subsistence farming. The farmers relied solely on the rains. These set in towards the middle of April and lasted till the end of July. This is not to say that it rained continuously during that period. They could, however, reckon with regular rainfall that would facilitate the growth of their crops during that time.

The average farmer began to clear the piece of land intended for cultivating in a particular year towards the middle of January or by the latest by the beginning of February. The first step in the preparation of the land involved clearing it of the thick bush encroaching on it. Father usually mastered that job alone. If the size of the plot to be cleared in a particular year was considerable and his financial resources permitted it, he employed casual labour on a daily basis to assist in the process.

The next stage involved the felling of some of the trees on the plot. This was necessary to expose the crops that would be planted to much needed sunshine. The farmers executed the job with their own manpower. The only instrument they relied on was the axe.

I could only wonder how father managed to fell some of the huge trees growing on some of our fields. At times it took him a whole day of sustained effort to fell a tree of considerable size. In some instances a tree he had attempted all day to bring down would still be standing at the fall of darkness. In that case he returned home and continued his effort the next day. Sometimes he received help from the elements during the interruption—a strong wind that might set in during the night to provide the final 'blow' to send the stubborn tree falling to the ground.

The next stage in the preparation of the field involved setting fire to the cleared bush. Before doing that, the farmer spent time preparing the periphery of the field with the aim of preventing the fire from spreading beyond its bounds. It was an important precaution, particularly if the field involved was bordered by others occupied with important crops such as cocoa, orange, oil palm trees, etc. One could otherwise end up burning cultivated farmland belonging to oneself or, worse still, to another farmer.

There were instances when, in spite all such precautions, the fire did indeed jump into other farmlands to cause destruction. With careful preparation, however, one could greatly reduce the risk.

Although very rare, there were instances when the burning of farmland ended in real tragedy, as the following instance illustrates.

Several years ago a resident of Amantia, the village where mother was born, left home to burn his farmland. He went alone. When he failed to return at the onset of darkness, his anxious relatives went in search of him. On reaching the field, the field was still burning. There was, however, no trace of their relative. Since the field was still burning they could not enter it to search for him. After searching the areas bordering the field in vain for him, they returned home. They returned early the next morning to continue the search. This time they could enter the newly prepared field. Their fears soon became reality when his badly charred body was found at one end of the farm. Surprised by the flames, he had apparently tried to flee but to no avail.

After the field had been cleared and the bush burnt, the next stage in the cultivation process was the sowing or planting of the crops. The farmers at Mpintimpi, as was the case in several parts of the country, practised mixed crop farming—a system of farming whereby several crops are planted on the same piece of land at the same time.

We filled our field with two types of crop—cash and food crops. Strictly speaking, only cocoa could be classified as a purely cash crop. All the other crops we planted—cassava, yams, plantains, various kinds of vegetables—served both functions, depending on the yield in a particular year. In a lean season we kept them for ourselves; on the other hand if the yield was bountiful, we sold part of the yield and kept the rest for ourselves.

It was all hands on deck when it came to the planting of the field, including those of the children of the farmer who were big enough for the assignment. The various crops were not planted simultaneously but one after the other. For example, the farmer first planted a particular crop, perhaps cocoa, followed by maize, plantain, yam, etc., until the whole piece of cultivated land was filled with the crops he/she wanted to plant.

As I just mentioned, the farmers' children helped in the planting of the crops on the field. In the case of maize, we placed the seeds in our pocket and went about, armed with our small machetes to plant them. First we dug a shallow hole with our pointed machetes. Next, we placed three to four seeds into the hole before covering them with soil. We then moved a step or two forward and repeated the procedure.

Depending on the size of the field, it could take several days to finish the task of planting one particular crop. Father trusted in the good sense of duty of his children. Children, children! Particularly when towards the end of a tedious day's job one still had a considerable amount of grain that needed to be planted in one's pocket, one was tempted to seek a quicker way of getting rid of it. Soon one began to fill each hole with far more than the recommended number of seeds at a time!

In the case of maize and cocoa, the 'day of judgement' did not take long to arrive, for the time that elapsed between planting and germinating was only a few days in each case. When father or mother on their regular inspection rounds through the newly cultivated field came across several maize or cocoa seedling springing up from the same hole, they would burst out in rage: "Who amongst you committed such treachery?!" As might be expected, each one of us kept quiet. They had no choice but to go round removing the surplus seedlings.

The planting process continued until all the crops the farmer set out to plant had been put under the soil. Sometimes it took him/her several weeks of hard work to achieve this. It was in the interest of the farmer to ensure that his field was planted by the middle of April, just about the onset of the rainy season.

The respite the farmer enjoyed on the completion of the planting of his/her farm was usually brief. With the onset of the rains and the springing up of the seedlings, another factor entered the equation. The rain and the fertile soil did not benefit only the plants useful to the farmer, but also the weeds. They did not only compete with the crops for nutrients and sunshine; some of them threatened to choke the crops also. To avert that situation, the farmer had to weed his/her field as early as possible.

In that area also, many a farmer counted on the helping hands of his/her children. That phase of the cultivation process coincided with the Easter holidays. Whereas our peers in the big towns and cities could enjoy relaxing at home with their parents, we woke up early in the morning, sharpened our machetes and headed for the farm. Sometimes we would eat our breakfast before making for the woods. On other occasions, the boys had to leave early with their father who usually left home early for the farm without even having his breakfast. He would usually tell us that at that time of day, his stomach was yet to awake from sleep! As long as that had not happened, he did not have the urge to eat anything.

The girls were left with their mother to carry on the usual early morning chores in the home—sweeping round the compound, washing the cooking utensils left from the previous evening, fetching water from the stream, etc., before joining us later.

After a tedious day's work on the fields, we returned home, around 4 pm. In our little village we grew what we ate and ate what we grew. Apart from the meat and fish we usually bought from the market, we relied mainly on the produce from our farms to sustain us. Without access to electric or gas cookers, we had to rely on firewood for our cooking. We carried the wood and the foodstuffs on our heads. To prevent the load pressing too hard on our bare heads, we folded pieces of clothing that we placed on the head to cushion it from direct contact with the burden being carried.

As in almost every aspect of daily activity in the village, we, the children, had in this instance also to help carry the items home. Thus, after several hours of hard work on the farm, the farmer's child returned home late in the afternoon with his parents bearing some of the load on his or her head. The situation was not made easy by the scorching African sun or the torrential rains that could set in to pound them mercilessly as they walked home, their necks almost breaking under the heavy load.

'Sow in tears and reap in joy' so the saying goes. Well, reaping in our case could not be described as a joyful event. With no machines to assist us the process could be very tedious indeed. Maize was usually the first crop to be harvested. In this case too the hands of the farmer's children were needed. Usually their duty was to go behind the adults, a basket on the head or in the hands, to gather the maize being harvested.

--15--
THE TREE THAT PRODUCES BLACK GOLD

A GHANAIAN LEGEND has it that once upon a time a Ghanaian sailor by the name of Tetteh Quarshie, while returning to Ghana from a trip to Fernando Po, an island off the coast of West Africa, carried some cocoa pods along with him. On his return he cultivated it on his farmland. Eventually other residents got hold of cocoa from Tetteh Quarshie's farmland and cultivated them on their fields. That marked the beginning of the cultivation of cocoa in Ghana. Though the above account is accepted by the majority of Ghanaians, a small number question the fact that it was indeed Tetteh Quarshie who had introduced cocoa into the country.

Whatever the truth concerning the arrival of cocoa in the country, it is an indisputable fact that cocoa has been, and continues to be, one of the main foreign exchange earners for Ghana. It is not without reason that some have coined the term 'black gold' to refer to the dark brown cocoa beans that even to this day account for a considerable proportion of Ghana's foreign exchange earnings. As at June 2010, Ghana was the world's second largest cocoa producer after the Ivory Coast, her immediate neighbour to the west.

Mpintimpi lies within the cocoa-growing belt of Ghana, so it is not surprising that cocoa played a very important role in my life. I was, as it were, born into cocoa beans and grew up with cocoa beans! Though as a child I did not understand the significance of cocoa beans to the country as a whole, one thing I certainly was aware of was that my parents relied on the income they obtained from the sale of cocoa to provide for everything we needed.

By dint of accident, Christmas followed closely on the heels of the main cocoa harvest season. The main cocoa harvest season began in October and lasted till around the end of December. This fact made it possible for my parents—and this can be said of all the cocoa farmers at Mpintimpi and elsewhere—to buy new clothes for their children at Christmas.

Though at that time tuition was free from primary school right up to university level, it is no exaggeration to state that without the cocoa beans, my parents would hardly have been in a position to meet the other expenses associated with their children's education—school uniforms and later the boarding and lodging fees of some of their children who pursued further education.

At the time I was big enough to understand my environment, father already boasted about five different small to medium-sized farmlands spread at different locations at an average distance of about two kilometres from the village, these being farmlands on which mature cocoa trees of various ages were growing.

In the preceding chapter I described how the farmer cleared a plot of land for the cultivation of crops. Cocoa requires a humid climate, a considerable amount of sunshine, regular rainfall and fertile soil to grow. It grows best with some overhead shade. The farmer took that fact into consideration when preparing the field meant for the cultivation of cocoa and left some of the tall trees in the field to provide the required shade for his future cocoa trees.

Under suitable conditions, the cocoa plant requires a period of about five years from the time of cultivation to the time of bearing the first fruits.

The cocoa beans are found in pods, which are ovoid. Each pod may contain twenty to sixty seeds or beans. The pods may grow to a size of between 15 and 30cm (6–12in) in length and 8–10cm (3–4in) in width with a weight of 500g (just over 1lb) when mature. Initially, the pods are light green in colour; when ripe they assume a yellow to orange colour. A cocoa farm filled with trees each carrying several ripe yellow pods ready to be harvested is a beautiful scene to behold.

The pods are harvested from the trunk or branches as the case may be with machetes or implements specially carved for the purpose. Harvesting is done by adults, usually men. Children, from the age of about ten onwards, went behind the adults as they harvested the beautiful golden pods from the trees and gathered them into heaps, each consisting of about a dozen pods. Depending on the size of the cocoa farm, and also whether the harvest was bountiful, the pods were gathered into several such heaps spread on the whole farm.

When the plucking of the pods was over, the next stage involved gathering all the small heaps of pods to a main collecting point on the farm. Usually the farmer selected one collecting point on each farm for this purpose. The helpers carried the pods in baskets woven from either the oil palm tree or the raffia palm, or both. The baskets, which were of various sizes, were assigned to the helpers, depending on their age and physical ability. Depending on the size of the farm, the number of helpers involved and also the yield in the particular year, it could take a few to several days to gather all the pods to the collecting point.

Next came the task of slashing the pods to collect the seeds. If it involved only a small yield, the farmer did the job alone with the help of his or her family. On the other hand, if the yield was considerable, the farmer invited other members of the community to assist in the process. The pods were slashed open with the help of a small machete to reveal the cocoa beans surrounded by the fruity pulp of the pod.

The whole content of the pod was then emptied into a basket. Sitting beside each basket was an assistant, usually a woman or a child, big enough for the task of freeing the beans from the pulp surrounding them. The beans were then gathered into a single heap on the broad leaves of the banana or plantain tree already spread at a location not far from the workers. Each heap of beans was tightly covered with the help of additional banana/plantain leaves and left over a period of five to seven days to ferment. After that period, the beans were carried home for drying.

When the yield was considerable, the farmer was not able to perform the assignment with his/her family alone. Instead, he/she went round the village to solicit the help of residents above the age of about 15 years to assist in doing so. The help offered the farmer by his/her neighbours was not a one-way street, for he/she could also be invited by them to help them transport their cocoa beans home for drying.

Once at home, the beans were spread on mats specially woven from the branches of the raffia palm for the purpose of drying the cocoa beans. The mats were not spread on the bare ground but on wooden structures constructed in open spaces at several locations within the settlement. These structures stood about a metre above ground level. Throughout the day, and at intervals of about an hour, the farmer, with the help of his bare hands or a specially constructed wooden implement, stirred the beans to facilitate the drying process.

It was the wish of the farmer to be spared rain throughout the period it took for the beans to dry. As might be imagined, this was not always the case, for the tropical rain could set in, sometimes at short notice, to disrupt the drying process. At the first sign of rain the farmer rushed to cover his precious beans. Sometimes the rains set in at a time when the particular farmer was not at home but working on the fields. In such instances, he/she could count on the assistance of whoever happened to be around at that point.

After about fourteen days of daily exposure to the sun, the beans were usually dry enough to be sold. The experienced farmer did not need someone to point this out to him. To be on the safe side, however, he or she chose to either take a few samples to the CMB or invite them to come and verify things for themselves. After the staff of the CMB had satisfied themselves that the beans were dry enough to be sold, they handed the farmer jute sacks specially produced for the storage and transport of cocoa beans. The farmer filled them with his precious beans and carried them on his head or shoulders to the purchasing spot.

The beans were sold in 'loads' of 60lbs. Usually the Government announced the price for a 'load' of cocoa for a particular year, weeks before the beginning of the main cocoa season of that particular year.

Father usually preferred that one of his 'young academics' accompanied him to the CMB. One could tell from the facial expressions of the clerk and his assistants that they were not amused with such intruders. Father was acting in line with the saying 'trust but verify', for rumours circulated that many a purchasing clerk and his/her staff took advantage of the prevailing illiteracy among the overwhelming majority of farmers for their own personal gain. They were alleged to declare a sack filled with beans weighing well over 60lbs still as a 'load'. Long after the unsuspecting farmer had left the premises, they would reweigh it and pocket the extra weight for themselves—or so it was alleged!

These were unsubstantiated allegations, of course—though the fact that the clerks of the CMB were counted among the well-to-do in society lent some credence to the rumour.

--16--
THE TREE WITH A THOUSAND AND ONE USES

IN THE FOREGOING CHAPTER, I dwelt on the cultivation of cocoa and the financial benefits the farming population derived from it. I would like to dedicate this chapter to a plant that also provided immense benefits to the peasants of Mpintimpi and elsewhere in the country, namely the oil palm tree.

The oil palm tree enjoyed one vital advantage over the cocoa tree. Indeed, while devoting much of our time and energy in the cultivating of cocoa, hardly anyone amongst us knew what the cocoa beans were good for! This could be said of the average cocoa farmer in the country.

It was only later on in life that I got to know that cocoa was used to produce chocolate, cocoa butter, cocoa beverages, etc. Even if anyone in the village was aware of this, what good could that be for us? Imagine a resident of Mpintimpi spending money on items like chocolates, cocoa spread, and beverages made of cocoa! Who would have thought of doing that when there was hardly any money for more pressing needs of daily life?

That may sound absurd to the reader, but indeed we laboured all year long to produce cocoa without affording to purchase some of the products derived from it. The situation was different when it came to the oil palm tree. Apart from the money the farmer obtained from selling some of the several products he/she obtained from it, he/she could also make direct use of some of the products.

Starting from the branches downwards to the roots, I shall provide a brief outline of some of benefits the plant brought to residents of our small village:

- The fibre from the leaves was used for brooms to tidy our rooms and our compounds.
- The leaves were also woven into roofing sheets to cover our buildings.
- The fibre from the palm branches could be woven into baskets; these, among other things, were employed to cart home from our farms foodstuffs, cocoa beans, firewood, palm fruits, etc.
- The soft oil pulp of the palm fruit could be used to prepare delicious palm soup.
- Still staying with the pulp, one could extract palm oil from it, which is rich in vitamins.
- The palm fruit contains palm nut. The nut, when cracked open, reveals the embedded kernel, commonly known as palm kernel. Palm kernel oil obtained from the kernel is also edible.
- The inventive human mind went beyond being satisfied with the benefits outlined above, it seems. Indeed, it has gone on to probe the plant for further possible uses. In due course, it was discovered that the 'Tree with the thousand and one uses' could also be tapped to obtain palm wine, which in turn could be distilled to obtain a highly potent alcoholic drink known locally as *akpeteshie*. (More about palm wine and *akpeteshie* in a later chapter.)

Despite the benefits outlined above, when I was young, hardly any farmer at Mpintimpi considered the cultivation of the oil palm tree. Instead, they relied on those that grew wild. They were indeed not in short supply, for they spread from place to place by several kinds of animals that fed on the fruit—squirrels, rats, mice and various kinds of birds. It was several years later when, partly as a result of unstable weather conditions and decreasing yields, the income from cocoa began to decrease, that some residents began to fill parts of their fields with oil palm trees.

The oil palm tree, unfortunately, is interlinked with a tragic family history. As mother used to tearfully narrate, one day my maternal grandfather left home to pick a ripe palm fruit. The palm tree involved was quite tall so he had to climb a ladder to reach the top. As he did so he suddenly lost his balance, just as he had almost reached the top of the ladder, and fell to the ground. As he fell he was pierced in his side by the branch of a tree. According to mother, he managed to walk back home, the broken branch still protruding from his body—but died shortly after reaching home.

--17--
ONE FRUIT, TWO EDIBLE OILS

AS I MENTIONED EARLIER, two types of edible oil can be obtained from the fruit of the oil palm. Palm oil, which is reddish looking, is extracted from the pulp that forms the outermost part of the fruit. Lying inside the pulp is the nut, which can be cracked to reveal a soft kernel embedded in it. Palm kernel oil, which is dark yellow in colour, can be extracted from the kernel.

The first step in preparing palm oil was to boil considerable amounts of palm fruits in a large dish for about half an hour. Next, the cooked fruits were placed in a large wooden mortar and pounded for several minutes using wooden pestles. The duty usually fell on the children of the home to carry out this task.

After pounding for a while, the ensuing paste was emptied into a large bowl. Lukewarm water was added to it. Using our bare hands, we stirred the paste until it dissolved in the water. The next stage involved removing the palm nuts, the outer cover of which is hard enough to withstand the pounding process without getting cracked. The mixture was then poured on a sieve to separate the orange-coloured mixture from the fibre of the pulp.

Next, the mixture was poured into a large dish and allowed to boil on an open fire for several minutes. Finally the fire was quenched and the soup allowed to stand for a while to cool down. As it did so, the red-looking palm oil began to float on the surface of the soup. This was collected using a large kitchen spoon. The remaining soup was then poured away.

If preparing palm oil was a tedious undertaking, extracting palm kernel oil from the palm kernel was even more tiresome. The first step in the process involved cracking the nut to free the kernel embedded in it. This was achieved by placing a few nuts in the hollow of a stone specially cut for the purpose and hitting them hard with a round-shaped quite heavy stone a few times until the nuts cracked to expose the kernels. The kernels were then gathered into a special container and roasted for several minutes over an open fire. According to mother, in earlier times they had to manually pound the roasted kernels into a paste. Thanks to a food-milling station that had in the meantime been set up at Nyafoman, we didn't have to do so any longer. The paste so obtained was placed in a large pan, mixed with some water and heated over an open fire for several minutes. After a while, palm kernel oil began to float on the surface of the mixture and was collected.

--18--
SIMPLE PEASANTS CRACKING COMPLICATED CHEMICAL FORMULAS

SOME WOMEN in the village were engaged in home soap production. Soap, the chemist will tell us, is basically the alkaline salt of a fatty acid. In other words, it is the product that results from the reaction of a fatty acid and a strong base (alkali).

How these simple peasant women, none of whom had ever sat at a school desk, none of whom had ever even heard terms like 'chemistry', 'fatty acid', 'alkali' and what-have-you, conceived the idea that they could produce their own homemade soap continues to baffle me to this day. Yet their method, though crude, was based on the same principle one would read of in any chemistry book—the same principle upon which some of the chemical giants of our day produce their trademark soaps!

As a first step in soap production, the women collected the pods that were left over after the cocoa pods had been slashed and emptied of their contents, as well as other materials such as skins from the plantain fruit, barks of trees, etc. These were left in the sun for several days to dry. They were then set on fire and burnt. The resulting ash was gathered into a large basin and mixed with water. The mixture thus produced was poured into a fine sieve and filtered. The liquid thus obtained was boiled over an open fire for several minutes until it was reduced to a paste. As a final step palm oil or palm kernel oil was poured over the paste, the resulting mixture being stirred at the same time.

Without any instruments to assist her, the soap maker at Mpintimpi determined by means of the experience of her eye when the soap-making process was complete.

Finally, the mixture was allowed to stand for several days to cure or to set.

The result, *Kokodoma*—also known by others as Africa Black Soap—can be used to wash clothes as well as the body. It is also said to possess medicinal as well as cosmetic attributes, capable of relieving rashes and skin irritations; also good for softening of rough and chapped skin, as well as facilitating the healing process of acne, blemishes and other skin problems.

--19--
THE IRON LADY OF MPINTIMPI

AS I MENTIONED EARLIER, palm wine is obtained by tapping the oil palm tree. In Mpintimpi and several places in Ghana, the tapper first has to fell the entire tree before tapping can take place. In other communities, the sap is collected from the cut flower of the still standing palm tree. During the first few days of tapping, the white liquid that collects is sweet and free of alcohol. The sweet alcohol-free sap is derided by many a lover of palm wine, regarding it as a drink for women and children. Indeed, when we were children that was what we yearned for. We either accompanied father on his daily tapping rounds to drink the sap at source, or else begged him to carry it home to us.

With the help of atmospheric and also residual yeast left in the collecting container, palm sap begins to ferment shortly after collection. Within hours, fermentation yields an aromatic wine of up to 4 per cent alcohol content. The wine may be allowed to ferment longer, up to a day, to yield a stronger, more sour and acidic taste, something preferred by the seasoned palm wine drinker.

Throughout the time I was growing up, father supplemented his income by tapping palm wine. Like most other tappers in the village, he did not tap only the oil palm tree but also the raffia palm, which is a variant of the palm family.

At Mpintimpi and also in several parts of rural areas of Ghana, palm wine is usually sold from makeshift huts built with bamboo sticks and palm branches and covered with sheets woven with the leaves of the raffia palm. The palm wine tapper's hut, as they are known, is in effect a kind of pub or drinking bar.

At the time I was growing up in the village, there were at any time two or three individuals who were engaged in palm wine tapping. It was not their main occupation; they only did so to supplement the earnings they derived from their farms. The palm wine tappers usually arrived with their produce late in the afternoon, at a time when the majority of residents had returned from the day's activity on their farms.

Palm wine is usually drunk from calabashes. It is indeed unheard of for the seasoned palm wine drinker to enjoy his drink in a plastic cup, for example.

Anyone below the age of about twenty was not permitted to drink in the palm wine tapper's hut. This was not a law passed by the state but rather a norm set and enforced by society. Whoever attempted to go against it could face the retribution of the adults gathered there. Though not permitted to drink there themselves, children big enough to do so could help their parents sell their produce at the palm wine tapper's hut.

I had a first-hand taste of life in the palm wine tapper's hut when I was about ten years old. Owing to an ailment to my left ankle I was unable to walk to school—a situation that persisted for two years.

In the course of time Papa Kwadwo Adu, a good friend of father's, sought and obtained permission from him for me to assist him sell his palm wine. For the teenager dying from boredom resulting from the forced interruption of schooling, the opportunity brought a very welcome change.

It was an unwritten law of society that only men were expected to drink inside the palm wine tapper's hut. Yaa Animah, a tall and well-built lady, who may well be described as the 'iron lady' of the village, seemed unimpressed by this form of discrimination of society towards women and appeared there on a regular basis to, as she put it, 'quench her thirst'. Hardly anyone she met there dared voice their opposition. The reason was not difficult to fathom—the iron lady did not shun confrontation with anyone, not even those of the opposite sex. On a few occasions she engaged some of the men in a fight—and prevailed over them.

--20--
"KILL ME QUICK!"

AS I MENTIONED EARLIER, palm wine can be distilled to produce a very potent alcoholic drink. The drink is popular not only in Ghana but also in several other countries in Africa. In Ghana the drink goes by several names—*akpeteshie, ogoguro, ogidigidi, kill me quick,* etc.

Father supplemented his income by tapping palm wine. He rarely sold his wine at the palm wine tapper's hut. Instead, he chose to distil it into *akpeteshie* before selling it to traders who travelled to the countryside to purchase it for further sale in the big towns and cities.

The distiller needed a special licence to do so, which had to be renewed on an annual basis. Father made sure he comported with the rule, though many a distiller failed to do so. Failing to do so could lead to trouble, however. Someone, in particular a business rival, could give the police a tip off, which could lead to arrest.

Father set up a crude distillery on one of his farms. It consisted in the main of three large metal barrels. The first barrel was placed on a large makeshift stove. This was connected with the help of a small iron pipe to a second barrel placed about five metres away. This served as the cooling receptacle. A third barrel served as the collecting receptacle for the tapped palm wine.

Usually he tapped several oil palm trees at the same time. He gathered the daily yield from those trees into the third barrel until it reached an amount he deemed sufficient to be distilled.

The distillation process began with the heating of the palm wine. The ensuing vapour passed through the connecting tube into the cooling barrel. To facilitate the cooling process, the tube was coiled at several places in the cooling container. The connecting tube ended on the outside of the cooling container. By the time it reached the outside, the vapour had condensed into the highly potent liquid.

Father usually had several different things to accomplish on a working day. He could as a result hardly afford to spend all his day at the makeshift distillery. Usually, after he had set the fire and made sure everything was moving smoothly, he assigned one or two of his boys who were big enough for the task to oversee the process. Their main duty was to replace the bottles in which the *akpeteshie* collected with empty ones once they filled up.

--21--
THE THIEF THAT STRIKES FROM ABOVE

WE RAISED LIVESTOCK at home, not on a commercial basis, but mainly for our own use. Out of her own meagre stock of poultry, mother from time to time entrusted each one of her children with a hen, not as a pet but rather to raise it for the benefit of all the family.

We were not particularly successful in our efforts to raise poultry. Several factors accounted for this.

In the first place we did not feed them as well as we should have. We had no idea of poultry feeds that we should have purchased in the big towns for our birds to feed on. Even if we did we would not have been able to afford them. We could have fed them on the maize we produced on our own. Well, we badly needed the cash we obtained from selling our maize so were reluctant to feed our birds on it.

Then there was the danger posed by traffic. Though the road that passed through the village was not particularly busy with traffic, vehicular movement was nevertheless sufficient to pose a danger to our birds, which we allowed to roam about freely during the day. Not infrequently some of our birds were run over by passing vehicles. On some of these occasions the poor birds were crushed to pieces in the process, to the extent that it was impossible for us to derive any use from their flesh. On other occasions, the vehicle did not inflict much damage to the body of the dead bird. Much as I lamented the loss of the bird in question, I rejoiced at the opportunity to enjoy chicken meat, something which otherwise was reserved for special occasions, such as Christmas and Easter.

Our birds faced danger that originated not only on land; they were also subjected to threats to their lives that came from the air. Our area abounded with crows that hunted our birds from above. The crows were a menace to our birds. They would appear in the sky, as if from nowhere, make a forceful dive downwards towards their prey, grasp the poor bird in its claws and fly away, just as swiftly as they arrived. The hunting expedition of the 'thief' from the air was executed so briskly and with such precision, it left the human inhabitants hardly any time for counter- attack.

The most serious threat to our birds came, however, in the form of epidemics that set in and threatened to wipe away the entire livestock. We did not consume the birds that fell seriously ill, or indeed that dropped dead. However, someone's poison is another man's breakfast, as the saying goes, for there were a few residents amongst us who enjoyed the birds whether seriously ill or dead! For such individuals, the bird epidemic ushered in a period of almost daily feasting on chicken meat.

It was heartbreaking to lose almost the entire stock of birds after investing so much energy to raise them. It was usually during the peak of such epidemics that word began to make its rounds to the effect that there was a veterinary centre at the district capital that we could contact for help. But who dared spend the little money one had to investigate a matter that might turn out at the end of the day to be a fallacy?

--22--
OUR AUDACIOUS FOUR-LEGGED COMPANIONS

SEVERAL HOUSEHOLDS in the settlement kept goats and sheep on a small scale. Hardly any of us kept them locked in barns during the day. Some keepers did not even have barns at all where the animals could be retired to sleep at night. Instead, the animals were left to sleep under the veranda or under trees within the compound.

The general practice was to allow animals to roam about in the settlement during the day. The animals seemed intelligent enough to return home on their own at the onset of darkness.

The sheep, generally, were easy to keep. Not so the goats! Goats are indeed stubborn creatures. Our goats, it seemed, simply did not respect or fear us! By their behaviour they often created the impression of having fun in provoking their two legged 'compatriots' into anger. You could spot them attempting to do something silly. You shouted at them to express your displeasure. Initially, they would pretend they did not hear you, taking no notice of you, but would stop their bad behaviour if you persisted. However, the moment you turned your attention to something else they would return to what they were doing and continue to commit the same offence—if not worse. They would renew the activity you had just moments before warned them against with renewed determination, it seemed.

There were instances when they set their sights on a chunk of food that a human being was just enjoying. By the time one became aware of their interest, they had already grasped it and were running away with it!

One did not only have one's stubborn goats to contend with; those from the immediate or even distant neighbour would come around to cause mayhem.

--23--
MY UNCLE, THE PROFESSIONAL HUNTER

FATHER DID ALL HE COULD to support his family, including hunting for wildlife or bush meat. He managed to acquire, under licence, a single barrel shotgun for this purpose. His heavy schedule of work on his farms prevented him from undertaking such expeditions, which were usually carried out all night long.

The situation was different for Kofi Ntrama, a maternal uncle of his. Kofi Ntrama, who had a room in the same extended family home where father lived, might well be described as a professional hunter, undertaking his hunting expeditions on a regular basis. He could not afford to purchase his own gun. Instead, he borrowed guns from a few of the residents who, like father, had managed to acquire their own guns. Usually he undertook his expeditions using a single barrel shotgun, although on a few occasions he managed to get some of the few residents who possessed the more sophisticated double-barrelled version to lend them out. The guns were lent on a 50:50 basis, the hunter sharing the prey equally with the gun owner.

Rarely did Kofi Ntrama return from a hunting expedition empty-handed.

Such overnight hunting expeditions were not without their risks. Reports of accidental shootings that took place during such expeditions made their rounds from time to time. One such report had it that once two friends who undertook an expedition decided to part company and try their luck in different parts of the forest. They agreed to meet at a selected place at an appointed time. Unfortunately, in the course of the night, the light being carried by one of them ran out of fuel. His light having gone out, the hunter tried to make his way back to his friend in the darkness. The other friend, sensing movement in the distance, thought it was some wild game and pulled the trigger, killing his friend instantly.

It was customary for the hunter who returned home with an antelope, or any game bigger than an antelope, to donate part of the meat to the Chief. He in turn presented portions to leading members of the town's development committee. The wisdom behind the arrangement was that, should something untoward happen to the hunter during an expedition, the duty would fall on the men in the village to go to his assistance. The community, as it were, expected a share in the hunter's fortune in good times against possible adverse circumstances in the future, when they in turn would be expected to assist him.

--24--
THE EXPERT GRASSCUTTERS AND THE RATS FROM GAMBIA

FROM TIME TO TIME, we undertook an expedition to hunt for grasscutters. Also known as the greater cane rat, the grasscutter belongs to a small family of African rodents. They can grow to about two feet in length in the longest individuals and reach a weight of about twenty pounds.

The grasscutter has rounded ears, a short nose, and coarse, bristly hair. They feed on grasses and cane; they also have a taste for cultivated foods, in particular maize and sugar cane. It is their taste for cultivated maize that prompted the most conflict between them and the peasant farmers of Mpintimpi. We would cultivate our maize or rice or cassava with much sweat, only to visit our farms in the morning to discover the cane rats had partied on our precious crops during the night!

We went after them assisted by our dogs. Indeed, without our four-legged friends we would hardly have managed to hunt them, for not only were they quicker than ourselves, they usually hid themselves under thickets almost inaccessible to humans.

On certain Saturdays, and also during the school holidays, after we had completed work on the farm, one of us would come up with the idea to go hunting for the Gambian pouched rat. Also known as the African giant pouched rat, this rodent lived commonly in hillocks and termite mounds. The Gambian pouched rat is omnivorous, feeding on vegetables, insects, palm fruits, etc. They hide in their homes during the day and at night venture out under the cover of darkness to look for food.

When we arrived at a hillock or mound, we looked for signs of occupation by the four-legged beings we were seeking. These included fresh claw marks left on passages and alleys leading into the heart of the hillock or mound.

Next, we looked out for all possible openings leading into the heart of the hillock or mound that might serve as an escape route for the animal we were after. With the help of the branches of trees growing in the area we blocked some of the openings.

Some of us would then take our positions beside a few openings that we deliberately left open. If, as was usually the case, a dog (or a few dogs) accompanied us on the expedition, it, or they, too, were made to guard some of the possible escape routes.

As a next step, we cut a long stalk from the surrounding bush. We inserted it deep into one of the openings of the mound and began to move it to and fro, so as to disturb the peace of its presumed occupant and so force it into the open.

Some emerged from their homes minutes later. We were either able to hunt them or they managed to escape. We would not leave them to escape without a chase, however. With the help of our dogs we were invariably in hot pursuit. Sometimes we managed to catch them; in other instances, we missed them.

What happened if, in spite our efforts to force them into the open, they remained stubborn and refused to budge? If the signs that led us to believe the hillock was inhabited were not very convincing, we abandoned our effort after a while and went on our way.

If, on the other hand, we were still convinced that it was inhabited, we took a step further in our attempt to force the rat to emerge from its hiding place, and gathered dried leaves that had fallen from plants growing in the area, heaped them at one of the entrances to the mound, and torched it.

Making use of a makeshift fan woven from the branches of the oil palm tree (the trees could be found almost everywhere) one of us fanned the fire. This was aimed not only to keep the fire burning but also help spread the smoke into the heart of the hillock. Soon smoke could be seen emerging from all the openings to the burrow, including those we had until then not discovered. The discovery of such concealed openings led us occasionally to suspect the occupant had perhaps already escaped undetected.

Usually it took a few minutes of fanning to force the rats into the open. If they failed to appear after a while we decided either to abandon our efforts or go a further step by cutting the mound open! That was a path that was rarely trodden, however. It was only in rare cases when the mound was small and the signs pointed convincingly to possible occupation that we went that far.

Sometimes we would shed much sweat burrowing into the belly of the lair only to find no trace of the animal we were pursuing. Had it already escaped? Had we deceived ourselves into thinking the mound was occupied? In other instances we found the animal already dead, suffocated by the fumes of our smoke fires.

--25--
THE BITING SCISSORS AND THE CRAWLING BEINGS

HUNTING FOR CRABS was a real adventure! The crabs found in our area lived in burrows in swampy areas bordering on ponds, streams and small rivers. Usually such burrows were partly filled with water that concealed their occupants. On rare occasions one might meet them in the open during the daytime. How were we sure a hole found in a swampy area that was partly filled with water was occupied by a crab? The answer is that they usually left their fresh footprints at the entrance to their hiding places!

After we had satisfied ourselves that a particular hole was occupied by a crab, we set about hunting it. Kneeling beside it, we slowly and carefully extended our hand far below the water level. Caution was required the moment one's fingers began to submerge in the water, for one could at any moment find one's hand in confrontation with the hunted. In real life, hardly anyone would allow an intruder into his/her premises without putting up a fight. Well, that was exactly what the crabs did! The moment they sensed the approach of our fingers they mounted a counter attack!

The crabs we hunted had five pairs of claws with which they moved about. The first of each set of claws is prominent. Not only are they prominent, each is shaped like a pair of scissors. The crabs used the two prominent claws to defend themselves from the human intruders. Despite their ferocious response, an experienced catcher could nevertheless hunt them without sustaining a nip.

That was not always the case, however. In instances not so rare, in spite of all precautions, one got one or more of one's fingers trapped in one or even both of the scissor-like claws. When that happened, the crab usually bit hard! Soon one could hear the screams or yells of the unfortunate victim! On some occasions, the crab bit so hard, it led to a cut wound.

Despite the hazards, we undertook the expeditions on a regular basis, particularly during the rainy season when one could be sure of a good catch.

On other occasions we went in search of land snails. These expeditions were undertaken not only as a means of supplementing our protein requirements, but also to earn some income from selling them.

Two kinds of land snail are found in the woods surrounding Mpintimpi; one dwells only on the ground, whereas the other is not restricted to land but can be found crawling on small and medium sized trees growing in the area. Though one might come across them at any time of the year, the main season for snails, especially the type confined solely to land, was the rainy season.

During the 'snail season' residents of the village undertook expeditions into the woods to look for the crawling creatures. Usually they hid under leaves shed by the trees growing in the area. With the help of our machetes we turned the fallen leaves, not arbitrarily, but at spots where we suspected the snails could be hiding.

At certain times the snails appeared in abundance. On such occasions, a resident of the village who was known for inventing wild stories began to tell the children he came across snails that had 'rained' down from the skies with the rains!

Going in search of snails was not without risk. The crawling creatures usually lived in moist and swampy areas. This turned out to be the kind of habitat preferred by another creature that could not be counted among our friends, namely, the python! Not only did pythons live in the environment preferred by the snails we were hunting for, but they also, like the snails, preferred to conceal themselves beneath fallen leaves. On some occasions one of us would turn over a heap of leaves hoping to find a snail only to discover, instead, a python! One can imagine our reaction at that moment—we took to our heels and fled as fast as our legs could carry us.

"As lazy as the python"—so a saying goes in the Twi language! Sometimes, after the initial shock, one or two of us gathered the courage to return to the scene to attempt to kill the serpent. Often we saw it in the same position we had initially found it—fast asleep! We then cut a long thick stick and destroyed it from a safe distance.

--26--
BE ON THE LOOKOUT FOR THE ANGRY SNAKES!

WE SET TRAPS on land, in rivers and streams. Broadly speaking, the traps we lay on land could be divided into two types. The first type was laid arbitrarily in the woods to catch an animal roaming in the forest, whereas the second type was targeted at animals such as grasscutters and rats that fed on our crops.

The one setting traps would look for tracks in the woods that would lead him (in the village, laying traps was exclusively a male domain) to conclude that he had identified a route being used on a regular basis by an antelope, a porcupine, a rat, etc. Then he would set a trap in a strategic place along the route thus identified in the hope of trapping the animal involved.

As I mentioned earlier, every year we cultivated a piece of land and grew crops such as plantains, maize, cassava, rice, etc. Some of the crops involved, especially rice, maize and cassava, turned out to be the favourite meal of certain animals living in the wild—the grasscutter being the most likely. It was heartbreaking, after all the efforts we invested in cultivating the land and planting our crops, to return to our farm in the morning to realise that, just as we were resting on our beds, the grasscutters from far and wide had assembled on the field, probably to celebrate a birthday party!

To avoid them reaping what they had not sown, we lay traps along the entire perimeter of a cultivated piece of land. This is how we approached the matter. With the help of oil palm or raffia branches as well as bamboo sticks, we erected a hedge that rose to about a metre above ground level around the entire perimeter of the farm in question. At distances of about twenty metres a small space was left in the hedge to allow for the setting of a trap. To serve as a further attraction to the animals we were targeting, we placed foodstuffs such as maize, ripe bananas or palm nuts at the mouth of the trap.

The traps were inspected on a regular basis, usually every other day. There is an unwritten rule that whoever goes to inspect a trap needs to approach the trap with extreme caution, for it could happen that instead of finding a grasscutter in the trap, one might come across a rat or a squirrel, or even a snake that was still alive and very angry!

We also lay traps in the rivers and streams in the surrounding area. Of particular mention is the Nwi River. We made use of traps specially woven from the branches of either the raffia or oil palm tree. Several of the traps were lined up at the same spot across the river. To prevent them from being carried away by the current, we supported them with structures we built across the stream. These traps, like those set on land, were also usually inspected every other day.

--27--
ORDINARY AND EXTRAORDINARY FISHING METHODS

ON SOME OCCASIONS some of us fished in the Nwi River. We bought the hooks and lines form the weekly market at Nyafoman. We used earthworms we found along the riverbank as bait. I was not particularly keen on undertaking such ventures for the catch was usually scant. With some luck, several hours of effort might be rewarded with some tilapia (or cichlid fish) or eels, or both.

Another method we employed to catch fish from the streams found in our area was known locally as *ahweye*. This method involved building a crude dam across two sections of a stream, at a distance of about fifty metres from each other and draining the section of the river trapped by both dams almost dry of water and catching any fish found in the area. Finally, both dams were broken to restore the flow of the stream or river.

Besides the Nwi River there were several other streams around our little village. Although the level of the Nwi River could fall considerably during the dry season, it usually maintained a strong current throughout the year, making it impossible for us to dam it by way of the crude means available to us. The situation was different with smaller streams, such as the River Yayaa, about a mile to the south, and the River Abomena, just about two hundred metres to the north.

The dry season was a favourable time of the year to undertake such expeditions. The lack of rainfall would have already led several sections of the stream to be almost completely (if not completely) cut off from the main stream, permitting us to empty them without the need to first dam them.

Mother was particularly fond of undertaking *ahweye* expeditions. Although not all her children shared her passion for that peculiar method of fishing, we usually accompanied her—after all, she had not only her interest at heart, but that of the whole family.

We erected our crude dams with the help of branches of trees growing in the area. These were cut and placed across the stream. The dam was strengthened with the help of thick clay that we collected along the banks of the streams.

Draining the section of the stream demarcated by us was an arduous task. Those involved in the undertaking, including children big enough to do so, took their positions a few steps away from the downstream part of the two dams. Armed with plastic and/or aluminium basins, trays, pieces of dishware, etc., and working together as a team, we sought to empty that section of the stream of water. Usually it took several hours of gruelling, backbreaking work under the scorching African heat to achieve our goal.

Our effort was not always rewarded, however! Indeed, on a few occasions we would spend hours empting the demarcated section of the stream only to discover at the end of the day that hardly any fish dwelt there!

It was not always an exercise in futility, however. There were indeed times when Heaven smiled on our endeavour, when our toil was rewarded with a substantial harvest of fish. On such occasions we returned home all smiles and prepared delicious meals with various tilapia, eels, crabs, etc., which we had harvested.

--28--
PLEASE FORGIVE OUR IGNORANCE

IN THE PRECEDING CHAPTER, I narrated how we laboriously drained segments of streams and rivers with the aim of catching the fish in that portion of the stream. The method of fishing I am about to narrate went not only beyond the ordinary, but also what was legal.

As I said earlier, the main occupation of residents of Mpintimpi and the surrounding areas was the cultivation of cocoa. The cocoa tree was not devoid of its enemies, namely insects that preyed on them and threatened not only their well-being but also the financial well-being of the farmers who relied on their crop yield. To counter the threat, the Government, which depended heavily on the foreign exchange earned from the export of cocoa beans, placed insecticides that were heavily subsidised at the disposal of the farmers. The main insecticide employed for that purpose was **d**ichloro**d**iphenyl**t**richloroethane—DDT for short.

Father acquired his own insecticide-spraying machine; the CMB lent them out to those farmers who were not in a position to buy one.

Father would first fill the machine with fuel. As a next step he poured DDT already diluted with the required portion of water into a container fixed to the machine. Then came the most exciting moment, at least as far as his children were concerned, when he went through the procedure of starting the engine. This was done by pulling on a special spring device attached to the motor.

One pull... *b-r-u-m*... came the response of the motor; another pull—*b-r-r-uu-u-m*.... the mechanical device answered, apparently not prepared to awaken from its slumber; it could follow another and yet another pull.... the facial expression of our Old Man would reveal the exasperation beginning to build up; then, finally, the all relieving pull on the string and... *b-r-r-u-u-u-m, b-r-r-u-u-u-m, b-r-r-u-u-u-m*... the motor sprang into action! That was met with the jumping about and shouting of the children of the farmer, who for his part breathed a sigh of relief.

Next, father fastened the device to his back and went about the task of spraying his cocoa farm with the pesticide. After a while he would return to either refill the fuel or pesticide tank or both. It could take him a couple of days to accomplish the task of spraying all his cocoa farms.

It usually did not take long for one to notice the change that his efforts had brought to his farms, for soon the plants began to blossom.

If only the farmers would restrict the use of DDT to the spraying of their cocoa farms! But no! Soon the insecticide was being employed for purposes it was not intended for—including fishing in the rivers and streams! It is superfluous to state that the practice was illegal and subject to prosecution. Those who engaged in it were aware of this and usually left the village under the cover of darkness to embark on their activity.

Long before the dawn of a new day, the group that had spent days planning the expedition headed for the Nwi River, armed with several tins of the pesticide. On their arrival they poured several litres of the deadly chemical into the river, and stirred the water at that spot to facilitate adequate mixing. Armed with machetes and containers to carry the catch, they followed the river downstream. It did not take long for the effect of the deadly chemical to be felt by the organisms living in the river. Soon the distressed creatures began to hop into the air and fall back into the river. Others did not have the strength to do so and just began to float on the surface of the river and were hunted down.

There were times when we left home in the morning to fetch water from the Nwi River, unaware that someone had undertaken a DDT fishing expedition upstream. On our arrival we would be confronted with hordes of dead fish floating downstream. We took advantage of the situation of course and collected them. Even as we enjoyed the fish, the scent of DDT was omnipresent. Ignorant as we were, we were neither aware of the risks posed by the chemical to our health (it could, among other things, affect the nervous system and also lead to cancer), nor the damage it did to the environment. In the course of time, not surprisingly, the Government banned the use of DDT in the country.

--29--
WILD HONEY FOR BREAKFAST

ON CERTAIN OCCASIONS we accompanied father to collect honey from bee's nests in the wild. Several weeks or months prior to that, he had discovered a nest in a hollow of a tree that was still standing, or that had fallen. Thereafter he visited it on a regular basis to ascertain the progress of the 'busy bees'.

Finally a time came when he decided enough honeycombs had been established in the wild beehive to warrant their collection. The venture was carried out under the cover of darkness. If he allowed his children to accompany him, he asked them to wait at a safe distance from the nest.

He usually torched the nest with a flame burning from a bundle made from dry palm branches. That permitted him to destroy most of the bees from a safe distance before he attempted to pick out the combs as quickly as possible. Still some of the bees managed to punish him for attempting to reap what he had not sown. Fortunately, he was not allergic to their stings so, apart from some pain he had to endure for a while, they could not seriously threaten his life.

Back home, we helped father to squeeze the honey out of the honeycombs. The honey so won was preserved in bottles. They were usually kept for home consumption, for what we obtained on such ventures rarely added up to any considerable amount.

--30--
ENEMAS AND SUPPOSITORIES 'MADE IN MPINTIMPI'

WHEN SOMEONE FALLS SICK, the first thought that normally comes to mind is to consult a doctor. That was not the case with the inhabitants of Mpintimpi. Several factors accounted for this.

The nearest hospital is situated at Nkawkaw, which, as I mentioned earlier, is about thirty kilometres away.

Many could hardly afford the transportation costs. Even if they were able to do so, finding the means of transport could be a nightmare. Most of the vehicles that passed the village did so in the early mornings. Thereafter, barely any vehicles passed until late in the afternoon, when the passenger vehicles that passed in the morning on their way to Akim Oda, the district capital, would be on their journey back home. Hardly any vehicles passed by in the night. Woe unto those who fell seriously ill at night!

During the time I was growing up, the vehicles that passed by were almost filled with passengers and goods, if not completely filled, by the time they got to us. To be able to transport the sick was another problem, for being sick and weak, it was often a challenge to sit in an upright position on or in such vehicles. On occasions we had to go on our knees to beg some of the passengers on the vehicle to interrupt their journey to make room for the sick! Usually they obliged. It was a laudable gesture, though, for there was no guarantee that the opportunity for them to resume their journey would avail itself thereafter.

Finding suitable means to transport the sick to the hospital was not the only problem that confronted us—finding the money to pay for the transportation cost and the hospital charges could also lead to sleepless nights. Though the hospital fees were highly subsidised by the Government of the day, for the poor peasants of Mpintimpi, it still amounted to a fortune.

Gathering enough resources to enable the sick to be brought to the attention of the doctors could thus end up delaying matters considerably. During the cocoa off-season, at a time when the already scarce resources of the rural population were even more scanty, the monetary resources of all extended family members put together would probably not come anywhere near the required amount.

The alternative for the extended family was to try and raise the additional money needed from the few well-to-do's in the community. The term 'well-to-do' might lead someone unfamiliar with the situation prevailing in the village to imagine a wealthy individual who had command over substantial property. Far from it! In a community of desperately poor individuals, anyone who in the eyes of the rest rose above the average level could be conferred that accolade.

It was when in times of need one approached such an individual to seek a loan that it became clear where the individual really stood. What the rest were not aware of was that the person was probably also suffering in his/her shoes, just like everyone else. Still, the individual might decide to stretch his/her resources in a genuine desire to help. At the end of the day, the money the person could offer would probably not add up to even a tenth of the amount required.

The bid to raise the necessary funds could lead relatives to travel to some of the neighbouring villages. Sometimes it could take several days to raise the amount required to take the seriously ill patient to hospital—assuming the patient was still alive by then!

As a result of these factors, in cases of ill health that were not immediately life-threatening, each person attempted in his/her own way to help cure themselves.

Many residents had some knowledge of various forms of traditional medicinal practices. My parents also possessed some knowledge in that area of human endeavour, having acquired their knowledge from their respective parents. Whenever they themselves or their children got sick, mother or father left for the fields and gathered the ingredients needed to cure that particular ailment. These were in the form of leaves, roots, seeds, barks of trees, etc.

At this stage, I would like to outline some of the therapeutic regimen of the traditional 'doctors' at Mpintimpi.

The leaves, roots, seeds, barks and what-have-you were gathered in a pot made of clay. Water was then poured into the pot and boiled for several minutes. (A clay pot was preferred because it was believed to contribute to the healing process. Dishes made of aluminium or steel were on the other hand shunned.) The ensuing concoction could be used in several ways: given to the sick to drink, administered as an enema, or used for a bath. The application in one form did not exclude the other.

Talking of enema! It was one of the most popular therapeutic regimens. Enema was applied to heal various kinds of ailments, abdominal discomfort, constipation, diarrhoea (running stomach), joint and waist pain, menstrual pain, inability of the woman to conceive—the list is endless. The components used to prepare the concoction that was applied differed from disease to disease, however. How many times did mother apply an enema either for herself, or for one of her children! Hardly did a fortnight elapse without one of us having gone through the ritual!

The ingredients could also be pounded in a wooden mortar into a paste. The paste could also be obtained by grinding the ingredients in a stone receptacle specially carved for the purpose. The paste could be applied as a cream on the affected part of the body. In some cases, especially when joints are involved, the paste could be spread on the affected part of the body and then covered with a crude bandage made with the help of leaves of either the banana or plantain tree. The bandage was left for about three days to allow the paste to achieve the desired effect on the body.

Some of the ingredients, especially those involving barks and roots of trees, were cut into pieces and placed in bottles containing highly potent alcoholic drinks. After they had been left to stand for a few days, the patient was required to drink small amounts of it on a regular basis.

This regimen was credited with the ability to deal with joint pains and rheumatism.

Some healers credited their formula of barks and roots stored in alcohol with the ability to cure impotency.

Finally, there was the locally made suppository-like stuff that was inserted into the body. Though not as popular as the enema, it was also a widely applied form of therapy. Whatever their composition, they were credited in particular with the power to heal pains of the waist, not a rare complaint among residents judging from the bone-breaking work they did on their farms.

Whatever their makeup one particular ingredient, namely ginger, was never missing. The burning sensation it caused to the local tissue was believed to favour the healing process. Others went a step further and added some pepper to help bring about an even speedier healing process.

Inserting ground ginger as a suppository was mostly for therapeutic reasons. For children, it gained an additional usage—as a form of correction! For boys, there was only one passage of insertion. The anatomical make up of girls provided an additional passage. Though this method of correction was rarely applied, the mere threat of its use was enough to call an offending child to order.

--31--
HEATING LEGS OVER BOILING POTS FOR A CURE

WHEN I REACHED YEAR FIVE at primary school, I was afflicted by an ailment to my left ankle—something that forced me to accept an interruption of my education for over two years. After mother and father had tried unsuccessfully to use their herbal formula to cure me, they consulted Papa Osei. He collected several ingredients from the woods, which, under his instructions, we pounded into a paste. This was applied tightly around the affected joint. To help keep the herbal medicine in place for a few days, usually three days, a crude bandage was made using the broad leaves of the banana plant. The therapy regime was repeated over several weeks.

After we had tried Papa Osei's method for a while, my despairing parents sought help from one traditional healer after the other. Some of their methods could be described as horrific, to put it mildly. Probably to ensure a more intense penetration of the mixture into the body, some healers first inflicted several cuts on the skin of the affected joint before applying their medicine, usually in the form of a cream. Since some of the ingredients included ginger, one can imagine the burning sensation I had to endure!

In another instance, the healer we consulted prepared a concoction of herbs that he brought to the boil in a large black pot on an open fire. Next, he took hold of a small razor blade and inflicted several cuts to the skin over the sick joint. Then he called for four young men in the neighbourhood to hold me firmly down. Finally, he grasped the afflicted left leg firmly and brought it in position close to the mouth of the boiling pot! The steam coming from the boiling mixture, he explained, did not only carry healing powers but was capable of neutralising the spell cast on my leg by evil forces. I screamed at the top of my voice as the steam burnt my skin.

"You have to bear it, my little boy; that is the only way I can help you!" he consoled me. Big drops of sweat covered my body as I screamed at the top of my voice. That did not deter him as he continued to hold on firmly to my ailing leg. Finally, after keeping me in that position for several minutes, he asked the young men to carry me back to my seat.

The horrendous treatment led to no improvement in my condition.

--32--
SELF-MADE DISPENSERS

APART FROM TRADITIONAL MEDICINE, we relied on tablets, suspensions, syrups, ointments, etc., that we could obtain from a few petty traders in the village or from some shops at Nyafoman. The most common among them were APC (perhaps a reference to the fact that it contained the components aspirin, paracetamol and codeine combined), as well as ampicillin, penicillin, paracetamol, codeine, aspirin, chloroquine, etc.

Thus after traditional medicine had failed to cure our abdominal discomforts, running stomachs, headaches, joint pains, etc., we headed for the homes of the petty traders and bought some of these medications. One may wish to ask the following questions:

- How could you be sure that the medication you prescribed for yourselves was suited for a particular condition?
- Being laymen in medical practice, how did you decide on the dosage?
- How could you be certain the tablets that were not being sold in their original packets, but in loose pieces, were not fake and also that they had not expired weeks, months or years earlier?

Well, we did not have the luxury to ask ourselves those questions. The fact, for example, that the APC tablet had in the past helped to relieve our pain was all that mattered to us as we tried them another time.

Two particular types of medication, both in liquid form, gained considerable popularity not only in our little village but also in many parts of the country.

The first was commonly known by us as 'Atwood'. It was a dark brown solution contained in a little bottle, about 200ml in volume. Atwood was credited by its 'fans' with the ability to heal almost every kind of disease—be it a running stomach affecting the child or adult; abdominal discomfort affecting a patient of any age and sex; nausea and vomiting in the child or adult; lack of appetite in the child or adult; or menstrual pain—one can continue the roll call of the diseases our 'friend' was credited with healing until the cows come home!

The second 'miracle worker', also a liquid, was light yellow in colour and carried the name TCP. Among the long list of conditions we thought TCP was good at curing were wounds (infected and not infected), abdominal discomfort, a bad cough, sore throat or loss of appetite. Some applied it as eye, ear or even as nose drops!

How many times did mother treat herself and also her children with either of the two medicines!

I recently came across our two most cherished friends. What did I discover? 'Atwood' in reality stands for Atwood's Laxative Bitters; TCP is a disinfectant! I began to laugh my guts out on realising that we took 'Atwood', a laxative that should be used for constipation, as a cure not only for constipation but for diarrhoea as well!

--33--
QUACK DOCTORS AND 'SMUGGLE INJECTIONS'

THERE WERE THE 'QUACK DOCTORS' who frequented our areas to treat various kinds of diseases. Only a few of them had in the past anything to do with conventional medical practice—maybe as healthcare, pharmacy, or ward assistant.

Though they carried tablets, suspensions, syrups, ointments, creams, etc., in their 'doctor's bags', they were best known for what came to be known as 'smuggle injections'. They took advantage of the prevailing belief among the general population concerning the effectiveness of injections. Mother, for example, always expressed her disgust with the doctors at the hospital at Nkawkaw, when, after taking the trouble to travel all the way there either to seek a cure for herself or for her sick child, she was sent home without either of them receiving an injection. On her return she would burst out:

"It was a waste of time, children, it was a waste of time!"

"Why?" one of us would inquire.

"They did not give us any injection!"

"Maybe your condition did not call for one!"

"Oh yes it did! I think the problem was with the doctor. He did not seem confident in the job."

"What has led you to that conclusion?"

"When I reported there last year with the same condition the doctor I met gave me an injection. This one was good for nothing!"

The 'smuggle injections'! One could indeed write one horror story after the other about them. Those who administered them were barely trained. The farthest some of them went in that area of medical practice was perhaps to observe a nurse administering an injection on a few occasions. Equally dangerous was their habit of using the same injection needle on several patients—needless to mention that they did not possess the means to sterilise their needles.

The medical artillery of most of them consisted in the main of chloroquine and penicillin injections. As far as they were concerned both medicines were capable of curing all the conditions presented to them by their trusting patients.

Paradoxically, mother, the avowed fan of injections, on one occasion, suffered severely from 'the side effects' of the injection she received at the hands of a quack doctor. A few days after being injected, a large boil developed at the injection site. Soon she was unable to bear any weight on the affected leg and it took several days of self-medication with paracetamol, ampicillin, penicillin and whatever other pain killers and antibiotics we could obtain from the petty traders in the village to restore her health.

When these methods failed and the condition of the patient persisted or even worsened, the villagers eventually resorted to taking the afflicted person to hospital. Even now I recall a time when Manu, my sister who is two steps below me on the family tree, was attacked by measles. Initially only a small amount of rash appeared on her body, but before long it spread all over her body. As usual, mother resorted to traditional medicine, but her condition worsened. She could hardly eat. Soon she became so emaciated she looked like a walking skeleton. I feared very much for her; indeed, I really thought she was going to die. Eventually, father took a loan to enable mother to take her to hospital.

Mother told us on her return how she received a dressing down by the nurses the moment they saw the condition of the severely ill child.

"You illiterate mothers! How long do we need to educate you in the need to seek early medical help for your sick children?!"

"It is not our fault!" mother retorted. "We do not have the money. Her father had to go round looking for a loan!"

"That is the excuse you always give! You usually get money for other social events, don't you?"

Deeply embarrassed, mother kept her peace.

--34--
DEALING WITH THREE MEDICAL EMERGENCIES

ONE DAY A YOUNG GIRL by the name of Dugiri, aged about ten years, was helping her parents on the farm when she accidentally slipped and fell on a sharp machete. She sustained a deep cut to one of her legs. Even today, I still recall vividly the speed at which blood gushed out of the wound. Following his instincts, her father tied a torque some distance above the wound which helped to reduce the blood loss.

As was usual in our little settlement, almost the whole village gathered on the compound of her home to show their support. We prayed to Heaven to send a vehicle around to carry the injured child to hospital. After waiting several minutes, a vehicle finally pulled by. After spending about a week in hospital, she returned in good health.

On another occasion as we walked home from school, four people carrying a middle-aged man on a makeshift stretcher emerged from a bush path that linked some of the surrounding farmlands to the main road. As we learnt from them, the man they were carrying had been bitten by a snake while working on his farm about one kilometre away. After tying a rope some distance from the affected site on his left leg, they decided to carry him to the main road in the hope of finding a vehicle that would transport the patient to the hospital at Nkawkaw.

Our ways parted, for we were heading in different directions. During the next several days, the scene kept flashing back into my mind. The question that preoccupied my mind for some time was whether they ever made it to the hospital. And, if they did, were the doctors able to save him?

Then was mother's close call! Though she had not been feeling well for a while, she decided, despite her poor health, to visit one of our farms to harvest food for the family. We did all we could to persuade her to stay at home—in vain. She was concerned that failure to do so would lead to a shortage of food at home.

For reasons that I can no longer recall, everyone at home found an excuse not to accompany her. In the end I was the only person who did so. We had lots of farm land spread at different locations from the village. This particular farm was located about five kilometres from the village. Towards the end of the walk to the farm I noticed a considerable deterioration in her condition. From time to time she was forced to stand still and pant for breath.

"You are not well", I advised her. "We better return home before things become too bad."

"You are right", she agreed. "Since we are almost there, however, let's go ahead."

Finally we reached our destination. She hurried to harvest some foodstuffs. Just as we were about to embark on the return journey, her feet could hardly carry her.

"Sit down and rest for a while", I urged her. She agreed.

After resting for about ten minutes, she turned to me.

"Help me get the load on my head."

"Let's leave it. The strong one will come and pick it up tomorrow."

"You help me get it on my head."

"But that may be too much for you!"

"Don't worry. I shall manage it. We have to get some food for the home!"

I sincerely wished I could carry the load myself! But I couldn't. Walking the distance there had brought about an intensification of my own problem. Mother remained adamant, so I had no choice but to help lift the load to her head. We set out to return home.

She could walk only slowly. On more than half a dozen occasions she stood still for a while to gasp for breath. The thought of her collapsing and perhaps even dying before we could reach home caused my whole being to shiver. Normally the bush path was quite busy, being used by others who had their farmland along it. On that particular day, however, the whole world seemed to have deserted us.

On and on we went with iron-willed mother unprepared, for the sake of her children, and despite the severity of her condition, to abandon the load she was carrying. Even to this day I cannot explain how she managed to make it home! Nevertheless, about two hours after we had set out on the walk home, we reached our compound.

"Children, you help me get the load off my head!" mother cried as she began to fall to the ground.

All those present rushed to her aid, just in time to get the load off her head, before she collapsed and fell to the ground. Before long she lost consciousness!

There is a common belief in our culture that just at the moment when a person faints, the indwelling soul emerges from the individual to set out on the journey to the land of the dead. It is commonly believed that the departing soul can at that juncture be persuaded to reconsider the decision to leave the land of the living for the dead—if people ran in all directions and shouted the name of the dying person at the top of their voices, saying something that might persuade the soul to reconsider his or her decision to leave. With that thinking at the back of our minds we set out to do two things simultaneously.

One group attended to her directly by pouring cold water on her (a common practice in the village, applied to anyone who fainted, notwithstanding the underlying causes), while the other run hither and thither shouting her name and saying things like: "Why do you want to leave us alone? Where are you heading for? For the sake of your children, in particular for the sake of Afia Serwaa (our youngest sister was barely three years old at that time) reconsider your decision to depart for the land of the dead!"

Owing to her generosity, kind-heartedness, sense of humour and plain talking, mother had grown to become one of the most loved residents of the village. The news of her illness spread like wildfire through the small settlement. Soon almost the entire village was assembled in our home.

Papa Osei was soon called to the scene. On realising the seriousness of mother's condition, he hurried for the woods. A few minutes later he returned carrying some herbs in his hands. At his instructions they were ground into a fine mixture. Next, he pressed out some drops of green liquid from it into the eyes and ears of my seemingly dying mother.

We waited anxiously for her condition to improve. To our delight she opened her eyes after a while and began to murmur some words, though inaudible. Despite that sign of life, her condition remained very grave indeed.

Father managed to raise a loan to enable her to be sent to hospital. We were faced with the problem of finding a means of transporting her there. After waiting several minutes, a vehicle heading for Nkawkaw stopped at the village. Our joy was short-lived, for the vehicle was filled to the last seat. Fortunately, some of the passengers, on seeing her poor state of health, volunteered to interrupt their journey to make room for her!

After spending about two weeks in hospital she was discharged home in good health.

--35--
OUR FRIEND FROM ABOVE

BEHOLD THE SUN, the faithful and trustworthy friend of the residents of Mpintimpi! He was so reliable in his daily appearance in the blue African skies that we coined the phrase, "As sure as the sun shall shine tomorrow!"

As I was growing up in the village, our good friend began his journey in the skies daily around 6 o'clock in the morning. It was just about that time that the inhabitants of the village awoke from their sleep and began to go about their daily chores. Around midday our powerful guest took up his position above our heads far above in the sky. It was at that time of day that we really began to feel the heat. On the farms, the farmers could hardly work.

During the dry season whose peak was between November and February, the effect of the midday sun was such that we were often forced to find shelter under the roofs of our homes or under the shade of large trees—so unbearable was the burning heat! After about three hours of scorching midday heat, temperatures began to drop a few degrees. At last our mighty visitor began, gradually, to bid us goodbye for the day. Finally, at around 6:30 pm, his traces could no more be found in the skies. Shortly thereafter a deep darkness engulfed our part of the world. To find our way in the dark, we resorted to our small kerosene-powered lamps.

It would be an understatement to say that we depended on the sun in many aspects of our lives. Needless to say, there were no machines for washing, or for drying clothes in our little settlement. After we had laboriously washed our clothes by hand we hung them out to dry in the sun.

With no refrigerators or deep freezers to help preserve our foodstuffs, we also relied on the sun to help us. Usually we harvested the foodstuffs from our farms on an almost daily basis and consumed them accordingly. When there was abundant harvest in a particular year, we sold some of the foodstuffs to some of the drivers and passengers of some of the vehicles that passed by. If some of the foodstuffs such as pepper, cassava, maize, plantain etc., still remained, we dried them in the sun for several days before carrying some to the food mill at Nyafoman to be ground up.

The powder we obtained from milling cassava and plantain were respectively stirred in hot water to obtain *kokonte*, which, like *fufu*, is also swallowed down with soup. In its turn, the powder obtained from maize was used to prepare *koko*, *banku* or *dokono*.

Perhaps the most important help offered us by our faithful friend was in the drying of our cocoa beans. We were told that in some countries the cocoa beans were dried with the help of machines. At Mpintimpi (and that is true for the rest of the country) we relied on the rays of our trusted friend in the sky to dry our cocoa beans.

--36--
OUR FRIEND BY NIGHT

IF THE SUN WAS OUR FRIEND during the daytime, the moon was our companion at night, at least during the time it was in its monthly cycle when it appeared brightly in the heavens above our little settlement. Especially during the dry season when the night sky over the village was cloudless, we could easily follow the twenty-eight-day cycle of the moon.

First came the nights when the village was engulfed in thick darkness shortly after sunset. In such moments, one might hear us snoring loudly in our beds as early as eight in the evening. The thick darkness stayed with us for about ten nights. Thereafter the nights became less dark with every passing day.

Just about the fourteenth night in its twenty-eight-night cycle it gradually became visible in the sky at night. A few nights after first becoming visible, it became semi-circular in shape. Eventually it assumed a fully circular shape. It was that stage in its cycle that residents of the village, especially the children and teenagers, had been waiting for! We took advantage of the 'natural electricity', as we termed the bright moonlight nights, and engaged in various kinds of games.

One of the games we played on such nights was '*Antoakyire*' which means literally 'it was not put behind you'. Though played mainly by boys, it can also be played by both sexes at the same time.

We all sat in a circle. One of us carrying a piece of cloth tied into a small knot ran behind the circle while at the same time singing:

anto akyire o anto akyire o
anto akyire o anto akyire
obiba bewu o

At the end of each line, the other players responded in a chorus

yie yie yie

The song was repeated as long as the player continued to run around the group. The player could do as many rounds as they chose. The rule of the game forbade those sitting in the circle from turning to look back. As the player ran, at one stage they dropped the cloth quietly behind one of the players and continued running.

The person who had the cloth dropped behind him or her had somehow to get to know what had happened, stand up and chase the first player. If that did not happen and the runner returned to meet him or her still seated the runner gave them a slight touch on the back. The seated player had at that stage to pick up the cloth and make the run. Their place was then taken by the first player. The game continued for a while until the majority decided enough was enough!

Another game worth mentioning is the popular girls' game '*Ampe*'. It can be played either by just two girls or two teams of girls. The players or teams are identified as '*Ohyiwa*' and '*Opare*'. During the game, the two players facing each other begin to clap their hands while singing and jumping. As they land each manipulates her legs, placing one leg forward. Ohyiwa wins a point if the left leg meets the other player's right leg, or vice versa. Oware wins if the left leg meets the other player's left leg, or if their right legs meet. The first player or team to score ten points wins.

--37--
"SOME ARE COMFORTABLY SEATED WHILE OTHERS ARE SUFFERING IN THEIR SEATS"

The community gathered on some occasions for an evening of Anansesem narration.

Anansesem refers to a popular series of Twi fables that centre on the spider. In such fables the spider appears sometimes as a cunning creature that attempts to hide the wisdom of all his fellow creatures in a pot so as to be able to dupe them in the end; at other times the protagonist is displayed as a mischievous being who seeks to play all sorts of tricks on his fellow human beings to get at their property. Ananse (the name stands for spider) could be tender-hearted, caring for orphans, widows as well as the poor and the neglected.

The meeting usually involved residents of all age groups. Indeed it was usually the children who gathered around the adults to request them to delve into their mental archives and come up with some of the fables stored there.

To prevent the narration from developing into a one-sided, boring narrative, the speaker would be interrupted from time to time by someone in the audience with a traditional chorus—*moguo*, as they are known in Twi. Everyone present who was familiar with the song would join in. After about three minutes of a musical interlude, the narrator would continue his or her story.

At this stage, I would like to present the reader with one of my favourite Anansesem fables, entitled *Ebi te yie, ebi nso nte yie koraa*. Translated into English, the title means literally: "Some are well and comfortably seated, while others are suffering in their seats."

As the story goes, there came a point in time when all the members of the Animal Kingdom gathered for a conference to deliberate on some burning issues affecting them, in particular those involving their dealings with their selfish, greedy, aggressive and unpredictable neighbour, the human being.

Bad luck had it that the frail Mr Antelope was conferred a seat right next to mighty Mr Tiger!

In the course of the deliberations, what Mr Antelope had feared from the outset became a reality as the wild feline neighbour seized every opportunity to heap insults upon him, even verbally threatening him with dire consequences if he refused to behave himself. The ferocious neighbour of poor Mr Antelope would not leave matters there. Instead, Mr Tiger gradually resorted to physical abuse in the form of frequent blows to the body of his weak neighbour.

What is more, Mr Tiger prevented his immediate neighbour from making any contribution to the discussions. Whenever Mr Antelope attempted to raise his hand to catch the eye of the chairperson, ferocious Mr Tiger would command him in a threatening voice to bring it down immediately or else be prepared to breathe his last.

Eventually a point came when poor Mr Antelope could bear his agony no longer. In one desperate effort to free himself, he sprang to his feet and cried at the top of his voice: "Attention please, honourable chairperson! I wish herewith to call for an immediate adjournment of the meeting!"

"Why?" the chairperson asked.

"Well", Mr Antelope explained nervously, "unfortunately the seating arrangement does not favour everyone; whereas some clearly feel comfortable in their seats, others like myself have been suffering in ours right from the word go!"

The motion was immediately put to the vote. It gained majority support, for almost everyone present had witnessed what had until then transpired between the two unequal neighbours.

--38--
A CURIOUS BOXING MATCH ON THE STREETS OF MPINTIMPI

TO EDUCATE THE POPULATION, especially those in the rural areas, on matters relating to disease prevention, healthy eating, family planning, etc., the Government of the day dispatched specially trained staff equipped with mobile cinemas around the country. On their arrival they gave a talk on selected topics and showed films related to the topic. As a way of enticing as many people as possible to the event, they usually ended the proceeding by showing an exciting film.

Due to the large area they covered, the mobile cinemas visited us once in a blue moon. Usually, the Chief was given a few days' prior notice about the event. He in turn dispatched the gong-gong man to notify us about the impending visit.

One can imagine the excitement that went round the village at the break of the news! All of a sudden, the upcoming event became 'headline news' not only in our various homes, but also in places such as the palm wine tapper's hut. At school during lessons, the thought of the approaching film show would occasionally flash through my memory causing me, if even momentarily, to lose track of what was being taught.

When the day finally arrived, my earnest prayer was that the rains would not set in to disturb the show. Sometimes Heaven did not act in line with our wishes—when, in the evening, the rains would set in and would not stop until late in the night or even early the next morning. When that happened, the event was usually rescheduled for the next evening.

On one of their visits they showed a film of a fight between the national boxing hero, Floyd Robertson and the Cuban national, Sugar Ramos. The actual fight took place at the Accra Sports Stadium on 9th May 1964. In what was generally seen as a controversial decision, Sugar Ramos was declared the winner. As far as his teeming fans in the country were concerned, however, Floyd Robertson, the local hero, won the fight decisively.

For the next several months, the mobile cinema team capitalised on the interest the fight had generated nationwide by showing the match wherever they went.

Several months after the actual fight had taken place, it was finally the turn of the inhabitants of Mpintimpi to see their hero 'live' on the screen. The excitement it generated was almost palpable. That night, hardly any of us could wait for the 'educators' to end their 'lecture' on personal hygiene and disease prevention and the other 'stuff'. Finally, the much-awaited film began to run on the screen. As it did so, the cheering and booing became so intense, one had the impression the fight was actually taking place live.

Much to the dismay of those who clearly wished the event would go on for ever, the time came when we had no choice but to disperse to our various homes.

As if the boxing thriller we had just then witnessed was not enough, I soon noticed from where I was standing someone throwing his fist into the air as if engaged in a fight similar to the one we had just witnessed. Those around him began to run from him.

What was going on? I began to wonder. Soon the reason for the uproar became clear. It originated from Kofi Adu, one of my cousins. He was about seven years old at the time. He had fallen asleep during the show. When his mother awoke him at the end of the show, he began all of sudden to throw punches in the air, in the process hitting anyone who happened to be near him. As he did so, he kept screaming at the top of his voice: "Damn you Sugar Ramos, I will teach you a lesson tonight! Yes I will show you where power lies!"

"Stop it, stop it, Kofi! You are not in a fight with anyone!" her mother tried to calm him.

My cousin wouldn't be restrained, and continued for a while to give all around him a 'sound beating'. It took a while for him to return to the real world—indeed, for him to realise he was neither Floyd Robertson nor engaged in a fight with Sugar Ramos.

From that day onwards, Kofi Adu's name became associated with the 'Government cinema'.

--39--
A WELCOME CHANGE TO A DULL EVENING ROUTINE

APART FROM THE MOBILE CINEMA SHOWS, another event that brought some variety to the monotonous evening routine of our little settlement was the arrival of the roaming freelance evangelists. Armed with their Bibles, these men and women of God, like the mobile cinemas, travelled around the country, in their case not to educate us on health and socio-political issues and to show us exciting films, but to preach the Word of God.

Their coming was not usually announced days ahead; instead, they usually arrived in the morning of the very night they intended to preach. The first port of call on their arrival was, as usual, the palace. After they had informed the Chief what they were there for, he instructed the gong-gong beater to pass the message on to the community.

Was it because of the change it brought to the monotonous nightlife of the village? Was it because of genuine interest in the message they conveyed? Whatever the reason, the event was usually well patronised—from the regular church-goer to those who rarely stepped into a church right down to the adherents of traditional African forms of worship.

The session began with prayer followed by the singing of a few songs. Sometimes some of the evangelists took time to teach us songs that were not familiar to us to enable us to sing along with them. This was followed by readings from the Bible, and then the actual preaching of the main message of the evening. The session usually lasted for about two hours.

Before we departed to our various homes, an offertory was taken to support the work of the roving evangelists.

--40--
THE DRIVERS' ASSISTANTS AND THE CHEEKY VILLAGE BOYS

THERE HAS BEEN CONSIDERABLE IMPROVEMENT in the transportation system of Ghana. At the time I was growing up at Mpintimpi, the transport system in our area left much to be desired.

For example, a journey between Mpintimpi and Amantia, mother's home village, a distance of about seventy kilometres, could take the best part of a whole day! One may wonder why we needed that long for such a short distance. The poor state of the roads we travelled on, and the fact that vehicles stopped at almost every village, be it large or tiny, along our route to allow passengers to alight from the vehicle and new ones to climb on board, accounted for the snail pace of our progress.

Whenever we decided to visit Amantia, we woke up early in the morning to get ready in time to hopefully catch one of the few vehicles heading from Nkawkaw on their way to Akim Oda. In all, about three such vehicles, each with official permission to carry about thirty passengers, passed by each morning on their way to the said destination. Sometimes luck was not on our side and we failed to find a place in any of the vehicles that constituted the morning traffic.

We went back home, prepared some meals and waited for our chance in the afternoon. That was the period when the vehicles that travelled in the morning from Akim Oda to Nkawkaw would be on their homeward journey. There was no guarantee, however, that we would find vacant seats on them either. That was especially the case shortly after the schools had broken up for the holidays, when Christmas or Easter was around the corner, or when any other important event that called for an increased number of travellers was taking place in the vicinity.

On not a few occasions, the family was left with no other alternative but to travel in smaller groups—we would allow some of us to fill the vacant seats while the rest of the group waited for the next opportunity. We had to travel first to Akim Ofoase, a distance of about sixty kilometres. Amantia did not lie on the main road but rather on a comparatively less travelled road that joined the main road at Ofoase. When we reached Ofoase, we usually had to wait hours on end for a vehicle to take us to our final destination. Although the area around Amantia is well populated, the poor state of the road discouraged vehicle owners from plying it.

With the onset of the rainy season, the condition of the road worsened even further. At such times it was not uncommon for potholes, in fact, veritable ponds of water, to form in several places on the road. Vehicles that dared travel in such conditions risked getting stuck in the middle of the road. When that happened, the passengers were obliged to join the action, using manpower to free the four-wheeled structure from the no-go situation. On a few occasions, human strength had to succumb to the powers of the elements.

When that was the case, the wearied human passengers were left behind with the vehicle while the driver and his assistant or assistants left on foot for the nearest town in search of a tractor to pull the vehicle from the mud. Those whose destinations were not far away usually elected to complete the rest of the journey on foot, carrying their luggage on their heads and/or on their shoulders. Others, who had several kilometres ahead of them, might decide to walk to the next town to seek some shelter and rest until they were able to resume the journey.

On occasions when we were not travelling with considerable luggage we chose to walk to our final destination rather than wait for hours on end for a vehicle that might well turn out to be already full by the time it eventually pulled up. When, on the other hand, we carried substantial luggage with us, or when, as it sometimes happened, rumours reached our ears to the effect that robbers had of late been tormenting travellers who walked the distance, we decided to wait for a vehicle.

There were instances when we found no vacant places in the vehicles that eventually showed up. When that happened we spent the night with friends and relatives at the junction town and hoped that luck would come our way with the dawn of the new day. At the end of our visit we usually went through the same ordeal trying to make it back to Mpintimpi.

The journey between the two villages was not devoid of exciting moments. The vehicles we travelled on were on almost every occasion filled with passengers and goods that far exceeded what was officially allowed. Even when at a certain point the drivers refused to allow more passengers on board, the strong and energetic ones, bent on making it to their destinations on that particular day, come what may, forced themselves onto the vehicle, at times long after the driver had set it in motion.

There were a few police stations along the way. Some set up barriers to check the passing vehicles. My impression was that the officers were more interested in filling their pockets with the 'gifts' handed them by the drivers than enforcing the law.

The drivers of such vehicles were held in high esteem by society. This was especially the case in the rural areas—not surprising, considering that hardly anybody there could afford even a bicycle.

One of the favourite pastimes of my peers and I was to run after vehicles that were packed to the last seat with passengers as these vehicles 'crawled' through the village, and scream at the top of our voices: "Sardine! Sardine! Sardine!" alluding to the fact that the passengers were packed like sardines in a can.

Such insolence on our part did not always fail to provoke a counter-reaction. Some drivers, infuriated by our cries, pulled their vehicles to a stop and sent their assistants to go after us with the goal of teaching us a lesson in discipline and good behaviour. On seeing that, we ran away as fast as our legs could carry us! Some of the assistants were not satisfied with that and relentlessly continued to pursue us. Having the advantage of being familiar with the terrain that in effect constituted our own back yards, we usually vanished from sight before they could catch up with us. Luck did not always smile on us, however. If our pursuers got hold of us, they gave us a sound beating.

One day I was travelling on one such vehicle when, all of a sudden, thick fumes emanated from the engine, to be followed seconds later by red flames. Soon the fumes spread to the passenger compartment. There were loud cries of "Jesus, Jesus, Jesus!" as everyone tried to scramble out of the vehicle which, in the meantime, the driver had managed to bring to a halt. Some, as they alighted, lost their balance and fell to the hard surface of the untarred road, only to be stepped upon by others rushing out of the vehicle. Fortunately, apart from bruises, lacerations and superficial cuts, no one was seriously hurt. It happened not far from the village so I could continue my journey home on foot. The other passengers who did not have Mpintimpi as their final destination came to wait in the little village until the opportunity arose for them to continue their journey.

--41--
THE HEALTH INSPECTOR AND THE UNKEPT ARMPIT

"**CHILDREN, HURRY UP!** Get everything clean and in order, the *Tankase* has just arrived!"

Full of excitement on hearing the news, everyone in the house leapt into action. One of us went to check on the large water barrel we used to collect rainwater that drained from the corrugated iron sheets covering the main building of our home. In the dry season, when it scarcely rained, we filled it with water we collected from the Nwi River.

Another went to inspect the large clay pot in the kitchen that served as a reservoir for drinking water. Yet another one of us went to inspect the small chicken coop at one end of our compound where our chickens that were left to roam about during the day could retire to lay their eggs or rest at night. The remainder of us went round the compound just to make sure everything was tidy and in order.

The coming of the *Tankase* was indeed a cause for commotion in our little village! The term *Tankase* is a linguistic corruption of Town Council. They were health inspectors sent by the Town Council to go round homes in the community to enforce the maintenance of basic standards of hygiene.

The inspector responsible for Mpintimpi resided at Afosu. Though we reckoned with his inspection tour of the village every four to six weeks, the exact day of his arrival was a secret he kept to himself. Beginning from approximately three weeks after the last inspection, we began to make preparation towards his next coming by taking extra steps to maintain the standards of hygiene expected of us. In the course of time some of us made it a pastime to create false alarms about his supposed coming. Returning home from the centre of the village, we would begin in all earnest:

"Get ready, everyone! The *Tankase* is in town!"

"Are you sure?"

"Sure, sure, sure!"

Soon it was action stations for everyone! To add credence to their assertion, the individual involved joined the rest of the family in the general clean-up. After several minutes had elapsed without any sign of the health inspector, one or the others at home would become suspicious and challenge the informer: "Are you *sure* he is in town?"

"Maybe he has returned to where he came from!" the pretender would reply jokingly.

"That is *not* funny!" mother would burst out on hearing that.

Recently, on a visit to Nana Tutu, a close relative of Rita, my wife, we were recollecting memories of our respective childhoods when the issue of the *Tankase* cropped up. In the process, Comfort, Nana's wife, recalled what once took place between a health inspector and a resident of her town several years ago. The inspector issued the individual involved, a middle-aged woman, a summons for failing to maintain the expected standard of hygiene in her home.

Such a summons involved the payment of a fine to the Town Council. The homeowner felt unfairly treated and began to protest vehemently. On seeing her teeth, which in the health inspector's opinion were unkempt, he threatened to issue her a further summons for that personal shortcoming. That made the lady almost explode with fury, for matters relating to personal hygiene were surely outside the health inspector's remit!

In her exasperation, the already enraged woman became even more exasperated and began to swear at the officer, gesticulating and throwing her arms in the air as she did so. The action of elevating her arms caused her armpits to become visible to the inspector. On noticing that she had probably not shaved them for weeks, if not months, the inspector threatened to issue her with a further summons—this time for her unkempt armpits!

Though they appeared to be a nuisance at that time, looking back, particularly from the point of view of a health professional, the *Tankase* played a very important role in society. In an environment lacking, among other things, basic sanitary facilities, a regular health inspection helped to prevent an already bad situation from deteriorating further and, in so doing, helped prevent the spread of disease.

--42--
FLEE THE TAXMAN IF YOU CAN!

APART FROM the *Tankase,* the *lampoo* collector was another organ of the state dreaded by residents of our little village. Their duty was to collect the poll tax for the district. One was expected to purchase poll tax tickets on an annual basis. From time to time, inspectors were sent round to check on defaulters. In this case, the responsible *lampoo* collector for Mpintimpi resided at Afosu. As in the case of the *Tankase,* his arrival was unannounced.

Probably aware that not everyone could travel to the district capital to purchase them, the lampoo collector did not usually issue on-the-spot penalty fines to those who could not produce valid tickets. That individual was expected however to have his or her cash on hand to purchase the ticket from the inspector.

Therein lay the difficulty for many a resident. Though willing at heart to contribute their quota towards the district budget, the inspector might have arrived at a time when such an individual was just not in a position to do so. In that situation, he did what was expected of him— by issuing a fine that had to be paid at a later date together with the basic tax. To avoid such a situation, those who had enough warning beforehand vanished into the woods and remained there until such time they felt it was safe for them to return.

--43--
A FEW POTS OF PALM WINE FOR DIFFERENCES SETTLED

AT MPINTIMPI, when one felt offended by one's neighbour, when problems cropped up between married couples, when quarrels arose between individuals or parties regarding land or other forms of property—in fact, when any kind of controversy arose between residents of the community—the persons concerned rarely thought of seeking redress before a court of law. Many factors accounted for this.

First, the magistrate's court was several kilometres away.

Next was the issue of legal representation. The nearest place one could find a solicitor was at Nkawkaw. If one was lucky to find one, the legal expert could be busy handling more important and pressing cases and would not want to become involved in disputes involving ordinary peasants.

However, the all-deciding factor that prevented residents of Mpintimpi and elsewhere in the countryside from bringing their disputes before a conventional court was the issue of money! How could anyone there think of spending money to hire a lawyer when that individual was struggling financially to meet more pressing needs of everyday life?

As a result, residents made use of the long-tried traditional system of arbitration to settle disputes arising amongst them. When anyone felt unfairly treated by another resident, the individual involved took the first step toward arbitration by calling on an elderly citizen they trusted to lodge the complaint. The elderly person, on pondering the matter, might decide to resolve the issue on their own without involving others. In that case they would arrange a meeting between themselves and the parties involved. After they had listened to both sides, they passed judgement.

If, on the other hand, they felt the need to involve other individuals of the community in the arbitration, they took the necessary steps to make that happen. As a first step, the elderly person informed the accused about the case brought against them and inquired whether they would be willing to appear before the elders at a later date for a settlement.

Usually the answer was in the affirmative, for it was (and still is) considered an insult to the dignity of the elderly person to turn down such a request. In a society in which the elderly are accorded a high degree of respect, hardly anyone would want to appear in a poor light.

Having gained the consent of the other party for a settlement, the elderly citizen invited a handful of other respected, mainly, elderly members of the community to become part of the arbitration.

A typical arbitration began with a call on the complainant to put their case before the arbiters. This was followed by a cross-examination: first, by the defendant, and then the arbitrators.

In keeping with the Twi saying, "Never rush to judgement until you have heard from both sides in a dispute", the accused was then offered the opportunity to present their side of the story. This was also followed by a cross-examination—first by the complainant and then the arbitrators.

As a final step, judgement was passed. It is common practice for the arbitrators, at this stage, to withdraw to a place some distance from the sitting to deliberate over the matter. It is usually said that they go to consult with the 'old man', the source of all wisdom, experience and good judgement, to seek his wisdom to help arrive at a fair judgement.

The judgement passed by the arbitrators was usually respected by both sides. Immediately after their decision was made public, both parties in the case were called upon to rise up and shake hands in the presence of all assembled as a sign of reconciliation.

Before the proceedings were brought to an end, the head arbitrator delivered a short statement. This consisted basically of words of advice directed not only at the parties involved but also to all witnessing the proceedings. (Anyone in the village who so wished could usually witness the settlement.)

For their services the elders usually demanded a token fee. This could be in the form of money, a few pots of palm wine, a few bottles of locally brewed gin, a few packets of safety matches, etc. The person declared guilty bore the lion's share of the cost.

--44--
MY SENIOR BROTHER AND THE NEIGHBOUR'S DAUGHTER

AMONG THE AKAN ETHNIC GROUP, marriages are sealed in the presence of key members of the two extended families involved. On the day of marriage, representatives from the family of the bridegroom call on the bride's family. In the presence of the future wife and husband as well as family members, the marriage is sealed after a short ceremony.

The bridegroom and his representatives do not come empty-handed but rather bring with them drinks and presents for the bride and her family. The presents usually involve money, items of clothing as well as articles like sewing machines, large portmanteaus, cooking utensils, etc. The Akan marriage rites are quite simple and usually do not pose a big financial burden on the bridegroom who must bear the larger part of the costs involved.

These traditional marriage rites have to be performed irrespective of the social status of the parties involved. That is the first step in marriage. Others could go further and officially register their marriages at the registry office and even later at church.

Failure to abide by this tradition could eventually bring the individuals involved, especially the husband, into difficulty. Members of the bride's extended family would look upon him as someone who had 'stolen' one of their members. Should the worst scenario, namely her death, occur, her family members could refuse to accept her body for burial.

Traditionally, it is the extended family one belongs to, not one's spouse that generally has the final word on one's burial arrangements after one has passed away. As a result, hardly anyone in a place like Mpintimpi would want to contravene the traditional rules and regulations governing marriage.

In former times, such marriages were arranged between parents and families, at times even without the foreknowledge of the marrying couple. Today hardly anyone, including any young man or woman at Mpintimpi or elsewhere, would agree to such an arrangement. Instead they seek their own darlings and future partners on their own—at school, in the church, at bars and discos, etc.

The first marriage I was privileged to witness at Mpintimpi involved that of Kofi Ofosu (also known as Emmanuel), the first child of my parents, and Abenaa Manu, the daughter of Maame Adwoa Adeye. Readers may recall that I mentioned during our tour round the village that she was our neighbour directly across the road, and also that mother and Maame Adwoa Adeye were close friends.

It was not surprising, therefore, that a close friendship developed between Emmanuel and Abenaa Manu, who incidentally happened to be the first child of our close neighbour. Initially, everyone took it to be nothing more than the usual kind of friendship that might develop between two adolescents. In due course, however, their behaviour led their parents and others to suspect that perhaps their friendship was developing beyond the ordinary.

At that time, Emmanuel had just finished a two-year apprenticeship with a renowned tailor at Akuase. Father was contemplating helping him to establish a small tailor's shop in the village. Following the rumours, father invited his eldest son one evening for a small talk.

"I plan to use part of the earnings from this year's cocoa harvest to purchase a new foot pedal sewing machine for you", he began.

"That is a brilliant idea", Emmanuel replied.

"I am not finished yet. I will also give you money to travel to Kumasi to purchase material such as khaki that you can sew and sell to the schoolchildren. That will certainly give you a boost in your business."

"Thank you very much, Papa—I am so grateful!" Emmanuel remarked, hardly able to contain his tears of joy.

At this point the elder man decided to seize the opportunity to confront his son with the rumours relating to his friendship with the neighbour's daughter.

"Tell me, Kofi, what is going on between you and Abenaa?"

"Abenaa…who?" my senior brother asked nervously.

"Abenaa Manu."

"Nothing, nothing, nothing! We are just friends, very good friends—nothing else!"

"Are you sure?"

At that moment Emmanuel hesitated a little before giving his response.

"I have told the truth, nothing but the truth. If you do not believe me, you may call her and find out from her!"

"You know I cannot talk to her. I can, however, talk to you. You are my child, my first born, for that matter. You know our custom demands that marriage rites should be performed by the future husband, before he and the betrothed can come close to each other—in other words, before they can consummate their relationship. I hope you are also aware that it is the parents who pay the expenses involved in the marriage of their first son. That would no longer apply should you decide to marry again, of course. As far as the first marriage is concerned, however, it is our responsibility to bear the cost."

Father paused for a while to assess his reaction. Emmanuel looked on, betraying a certain amount of unease by the expression on his face.

"Now I want you to choose between two options", Father went on. "Either you signal me to go ahead and invest in your tailoring business, or tell me to save the money for the marriage rites that will need to be performed in your forthcoming marriage to your 'wife-to-be', Abenaa Manu!"

"Who told you she is my 'wife'! You take my word for it—we are no more than friends, ordinary friends."

"So I should go ahead and invest in your business?"

"Yes, of course."

"You promise that you will maintain a safe distance from Abenaa?"

"You have my promise!"

True to his word, at the peak of the cocoa harvest season, father left home early one morning, accompanied by his first child, to travel to Kumasi, Ghana's second largest city, a little over 100 kilometres to the north of the village.

They returned late in the evening with a brand new Singer foot pedal sewing machine as well as two large cotton carrier sacks packed to the hilt with several pieces of yet to be sewn cotton material of various designs and colours. Besides that, father also gave him a lump sum to meet the initial cost of running his business.

Emmanuel was a canny young man. Having been put on a firm business footing by his caring old man, he began to intensify, rather than withdraw, from his friendship with the attractive young woman on the other side of the road, in spite of what he had promised his father.

In due course Abenaa's mother began to notice a change in the physical appearance of her daughter. "Tell me, what has Koo Tano (using my brother's alias) been doing to you?!" In the end, she let the cat out of the bag. In those days, it was generally expected that the marriage rites were performed before a woman and a man got too close to one another. To avoid any embarrassment to both families, representatives from both sides soon gathered to perform the traditional marriage rites. Several months later, Amma, who was later christened Alice, was born.

--45--
THE SAD END TO A PROMISING ROMANCE

IN THE SAME WAY that the traditional marriage is sealed before representatives from the extended families of the two individuals involved, tradition requires that divorce be carried out in the presence of witnesses from the extended families of both parties involved.

Usually great effort is made to save marriages from collapsing. This generally involves arbitration (which I touched on earlier) but if, in spite of all such efforts to save the marriage, those involved opt for divorce, representatives of both families come together to dissolve the union.

Sadly, the first divorce I experienced as a child also involved a close member of the family—guess who? Emmanuel! Unfortunately, his marriage to my sister-in- law got into difficulty only a few years after it had been sealed. The climax to the simmering problems in the marriage came when he decided to take a second wife.

Emmanuel was a victim of the prevailing environment, for at that time polygamy was a common practice. Many a first wife, while not agreeing with it, was forced to live with it. My self-confident and strong-willed sister-in-law was uncompromising in the matter. However, Emmanuel on his part decided to stick to his decision.

Thus, barely ten years after they came together to seal the union, the extended family members of the two individuals gathered to dissolve it. The breakdown of the marriage, as might be expected, led to tensions between the two families on each side of the road. It was a very unfortunate situation, for we were very intricately linked with one another, like one big family, sharing almost everything with one another.

Fortunately the strong bond of friendship between the two families was able to withstand the tension. After the initial irritation, relations got back to normal. In the end the two directly affected individuals, both of whom have in the meantime passed away, became very good friends and remained so till the end.

During my last visit to the village in 2009, I did not meet any man who had more than one wife. That reflects a trend that can be observed throughout the country.

Several factors account for this. The first is the free education policy initiated by Dr Nkrumah's regime in 1961. Many an educated and enlightened woman will not want to share her husband with a second wife.

The high cost of living in the country has also made many a man reluctant to take on a second wife.

The third and most important factor is the spread of Christianity in the country in the recent past.

--46--
THE WAILING GRANDCHILDREN

IN OUR SOCIETY it is the community as a whole that buries the dead. This is particularly true in a small village such as Mpintimpi. When one of their members passes away, the whole community gets involved in the preparations towards the burial and the funeral celebrations that follow.

Shortly after the death of a resident of the settlement, a delegation from the extended family of the deceased calls on the Chief, the traditional custodian of the land, to break the news and at the same time seek his consent to bury the dead on the land under his custody. Seeking the consent of the Chief in such a manner is, strictly speaking, only a traditional formality. Usually every extended family or clan is apportioned land by the Chief where they bury their dead.

The Chief in turn summons the *Nkwaakwaahene,* the sub-chief directly responsible for the affairs of the youth and young adults of the community, and entrusts him with the task of organising them to dig a suitable grave.

The deceased is laid in state in the night prior to the day of burial. The lying in state usually lasts well into the latter part of the afternoon of the following day. Finally, long before the fall of darkness, the deceased person is carried by able-bodied men to its final resting place. There were two different cemeteries in the village—one for Christians and another for non-Christians.

As a child, I was scared beyond measure whenever someone in the little settlement passed away. As I have mentioned on several occasions, the community was like a big family where each knew the other. During the next several days after the sad event the thought that I could perhaps come into direct confrontation with the ghost of the dead frightened me to the bones!

The first funeral I witnessed as a child involved that of my great-grandmother Nana Adwoa Serwaah, father's maternal grandmother. Tradition requires that on such occasions, the grandchildren (and the great-grandchildren as the case may be) join together in a group to pay their last respect to the dead. With our mourning clothes wrapped around our bodies and each of us carrying a thin stalk as tall as ourselves, we stamped the earth in accord with the stem. As we did so we sang several times over the chorus:

Nana due due, Yaa Nana Oh!
Nana due due, Yaa Nana Oh!
Nana wode yen gyaa hwan ni oh?

(Fare thee well Grandpa/Grandma; who should take care of us in your absence?)

--47--
A RARE TRAGIC HAPPENING IN A SERENE ENVIRONMENT

ONE EVENING, when I was about ten years old, word began to spread in the little community to the effect that one of the residents had not returned home from work on his farm.

It was not typical of the generally quiet, decent and hard-working individual involved. Originally from the northern region of the country, he had moved with his wife to settle in the village several years before. Although at the time of their arrival, they could hardly speak the local Twi language, both of them had in the meantime made considerable progress in that respect and were well integrated in the community.

He earned his living as a casual labourer mostly on a day-to-day basis, helping the peasants clear their land, harvest their produce, carry the produce home, etc. Father had on several occasions engaged him on his farmland.

As I mentioned earlier, their humble dwelling was the first compound on the right-hand-side of the road approaching the village from Nkawkaw. By virtue of the close proximity of their home to ours, a bond of friendship had developed between them and us. On numerous occasions, either Kofi Dagarti himself, or his wife Adwoa Dagarti came over to our compound either to just chat with us or, in some instances, beg mother for foodstuffs. Mother, if she was in a position to help, did not hesitate in doing so.

We all wondered what was preventing him from returning from the fields. As is usual in the rural communities of the country, particularly those situated far from a police station, when something of this nature happens, it is the Chief of the area who is the first port of call. Thus the man's concerned wife soon contacted the Chief to inform him about the matter.

Soon the sound of the gong-gong filled the evening air as the gong-gong beater beat his gong to summon all the able-bodied men in the community to report to the palace without delay. Minutes later most of the men in the community were heading for the palace.

Moments later, a search party was dispatched to look for the missing man. Divided into several search teams, the men headed for all possible locations they suspected he might have visited. The teams returned at nightfall without finding any trace of the missing man. The search continued the whole of the next day, still without any success.

On the third day, just around midday, one of the teams was seen heading back to the village. The countenance on their faces spoke reams. Everyone was anxious to know what had happened. They kept their silence, though, for tradition demanded that any news they were conveying should first be broken to the Chief.

Soon almost the entire village assembled in the court of the palace. Finally, the leader of the group began:

"Nana, I wish I could be conveying delightful news. Unfortunately, that is not the case. Indeed, it is with great sadness that I report that we have found him. Unfortunately none of us could help him; for we found him hanging from a tree about half a mile from the village."

Hardly anyone present could hide his or her tears on hearing this dreadful news. Committing suicide was almost unheard of in the community. Indeed, no one, not even the very aged, could recall the last time something of that nature happened in our little settlement.

After a while, the Chief added to his words, speaking through his linguist (tradition does not allow the Chief to speak directly to his subjects; he does so only through his linguist), he began:

"It is indeed heartbreaking to learn that something of this nature has taken place in our community. We all can only wonder what led him to such an act of desperation. Well, we ordinary humans cannot undo what death has done. What we can do however is to stand by Adwoa in this, her very difficult moments. I do urge you all to not only pray for her, but show concrete love, visiting her to keep her company." He paused for a while as if to regain his composure. He continued after a while:

"As you may be aware, the law requires us to inform the police as soon as possible. I will therefore without delay send a messenger to Afosu to inform the police about what has happened.

"They will have to decide what to do with the body. As it is our custom, however, the body of this person, when it is released, will not be laid in state. As far as possible when it comes to the time to bury him, the funeral procession should avoid passing through the settlement, for it is an abomination for such a body to have any contact with the settlement."

Indeed, the Akans consider it an abomination for a person who commits suicide to be laid in state. The same applies to other deaths that occur through tragic circumstances, such as when a woman dies delivering her baby. (In such a case, society believes that laying the body in state can serve as a bad omen for other women attempting to deliver their children.)

Eventually the police collected the body of the deceased. It was taken to the hospital at Nkawkaw where a post-mortem was conducted, before being returned to the village for burial.

As might be expected, Adwoa Dagarti was devastated by the tragic event. Society did its best to stand by her. Several months after the death of her husband, she left the little settlement and headed back to her home town, never to return.

--48--
ABANDONED WHEEL RIMS AS CHURCH BELLS

AT THE TIME I was growing up at Mpintimpi, Christianity was the main form of worship for the great majority of residents. The rest of the population were adherents of various forms of traditional African worship. Though at that time about twenty per cent of the population of Ghana were Muslims, they, as I mentioned earlier, lived mostly in the north of the country.

There were two churches in the village: the Presbyterian as well as the Apostolic Church, the Presbyterian Church being the larger of the two in terms of the average Sunday attendance.

I still remember the church bell of the Presbyterian Church. It was not the type of church bell one would usually associate with a church—as in several aspects of life, the inhabitants had to improvise.

The main component of the bell was the metal rim of the wheel of an abandoned vehicle. With the help of a metal chain, the rim was hung on a supporting wooden structure that rose to about a metre above the ground. It stood about fifty metres away from the church building. The bell was sounded with the help of a piece of iron rod, about twenty centimetres long.

Later, when a primary school was built in the village, it also served as the bell that signalled the beginning of the school day.

Although anyone in the church could be called upon to sound the bell, the duty was usually entrusted to one particular teenage boy at a time.

The Sunday worship service of the Presbyterian Church, 'Presby' for short, began at 10 am. The first bell sounded at 8 am, to be followed an hour later by the second. In each case, it lasted for about five minutes.

Papa Teacher, the pastor of the Presby Church, was particularly punctual. He usually left home at 9:45 am for the approximately five-minute walk to the church. Shortly before he did so, he sent someone to instruct the 'bell boy' to sound the third and last bell. At the sound of the third bell, whoever wanted to be in church that morning had to hurry, for Papa Teacher hated it when worshippers turned up late to disturb the proceedings.

It was customary for churches in Ghana to organise a once yearly Harvest and Fundraising Day Service to raise additional funds to support their activities. The little Presbyterian Church at Mpintimpi was no exception. Several weeks prior to the event, they sent out envelopes to every household in the community and also the surrounding villages—Christian or non-Christian—everyone was called upon to donate money to support God's work.

On Harvest and Fundraising Day, members of the congregation carried various items to church, usually the best produce from their farms or livestock—yams, plantains, pineapples, oranges, fowl eggs, etc. The service was attended not only by members of the congregation, but by the community at large. Usually, a well-to- do member of the community was invited to chair the function.

The items donated by members were auctioned and the proceeds kept in the coffers of the church to support its activities.

Looking back, I can only wonder how far the poor peasants were prepared to go in terms of financial sacrifice to ensure the smooth running of their church.

The Presby Church had a singing band, a kind of choir. On occasions such as Christmas and Easter, they made a procession through the main street of the village and filled the air with inspiring gospel songs.

--49--
CHRISTMAS CAROLS FOR BISCUITS

AT THE TIME I WAS GROWING UP in little Mpintimpi, Christmas was generally referred to as 'a festival for children'. This was because it was usually at that time of the year that many parents managed to afford to purchase new clothes for their children.

By coincidence, Christmas occurs about the same time as the major cocoa- harvesting season. This placed many parents in a position to present their children with new clothes to celebrate the occasion.

That was not the case for all, however. A number of factors—a poor harvest, illness that called for hospitalisation that could drain scarce resources, the death of a family member, which could place a financial strain on the household, for example—could shatter the long-cherished hopes of children to be presented with new clothes to wear for the occasion.

The term 'new clothes' could be misleading. It could for example lead the stranger to our environment to imagine it referred to items like a shirt of the best brand, a designer coat, a cute pair of trousers, an admirable pair of shoes of the best brand, etc. That was not the case, for our parents could not afford luxuries. We had instead to content ourselves with pieces of cotton clothing known locally as *ntama*. Each child in our village usually received a piece of *ntama* to mark the occasion. Shoes to accompany the piece of clothing were out of the question.

26th December (appropriately, Boxing Day!) was a special day for the children of Mpintimpi, for it was on that day that we received our long-awaited new *ntama*.

A stranger to the village, at least on the 26th of December, would have little difficulty figuring out which of the several children that assembled on the streets shared the same parents, for it was the practice of parents to present their children with the same type of *ntama* for the occasion.

If only for the sake of being seen, almost every child in the village attended church that day. After service we went in small groups from house to house singing Christmas carols. In return we were usually given biscuits.

Christmas also offered us the opportunity to enjoy rich meals cooked with rice, chicken, mutton and beef—something we could only dream of on an ordinary day.

It is customary to share food prepared at Christmas with relatives, friends and neighbours. They are not invited home; instead, they are sent portions of the meal in small bowls and dishes. The duty falls on the children to carry out such deliveries.

Mother was especially kind-hearted. Particularly at Christmas, she sought to share our meal with as many as possible. The result was that we were often left with little meat for ourselves. We had waited all year long for the opportunity to enjoy our delicacies, only to feel short-changed when the time finally arrived!

--50--
POCKET MONEY EARNED THE HARD WAY

I DID NOT RECEIVE ANY POCKET MONEY from our parents; the same could be said of every child growing up in our community. When we were big enough to do so, we found avenues by which we could earn some money for ourselves. One important avenue open to us was through the sale of kola nuts.

Apart from cultivating cocoa, a few residents of the village reserved part of their land for the cultivation of kola nut trees. The kola nut tree, which thrives in tropical climates, can attain a height of about 20 metres. It boasts glossy ovoid leaves and bears fruits that can contain several nuts. The kola nut has a bitter flavour and contains caffeine.

Chewing kola nuts is not popular with the population of southern Ghana. The situation is different among the tribes in the north of the country as well as other inhabitants of the west African sub-region, in particular Nigeria.

There is something about the kola tree that is not found with the cocoa tree. The cocoa fruit, also known as pods, when ripe will remain on the tree or its branches as the case may be, until it is harvested. It goes rotten on the tree if that does not happen. The situation is different with the kola fruit—it has the tendency to fall to the ground on reaching maturity, and is left unharvested for a while. The rain and also wind favour this process.

The children in the village, and to some extent some adults, capitalised on this fact and got up early in the morning and visited the various kola farms in and around the village looking for fruits that might have fallen down during the night.

"That amounted to reaping what you had not sown!" someone might point out. While not disputing this, I would like to explain that our society did not consider it an offence to do so. Usually the farmers waited for the most favourable time, a time when several fruits had simultaneously reached maturity, to harvest their crop. Hardly any of them were prepared to visit their farms on a daily basis to look for fruits that had dropped down overnight.

What we were not permitted to do was to actively pluck the fruits from the trees ourselves. Whoever was caught by a landowner doing so had to accept the consequences. If it involved a child or a teenager, the landowner might decide to deal with them themselves. In that case, the landowner would probably cut a stalk from the bush and give them a whipping! If, on the other hand, the offender was an adult, the owner brought them before arbitration.

The kola nuts were sold to traders who bought them for sale in the northern part of the country, as well as Nigeria and other parts of west Africa. Usually they were sold in quantities of hundreds; the price for a hundred kola nuts fluctuated considerably, depending on the time of year and also whether the harvest was abundant or meagre.

Another way we earned pocket money was to perform various kinds of odd jobs. One of the common ones involved clearing cocoa farms of weeds prior to the cocoa harvest. To the person not conversant with cocoa farming this may appear to be a job too difficult for teenagers to master. Well, compared to other activities such as clearing a virgin or secondary forest in preparation for its cultivation, weeding under mature cocoa trees was quite easy, even for children of our age. Usually the leaves of mature cocoa trees form a canopy that prevents sufficient sunlight from reaching the ground beneath them. As a result, not much by way of undergrowth results, making it easy to weed those areas. We usually performed such jobs during the holidays, either on days when our parents were engaged in communal labour or when an event such as a funeral celebration prevented us from working on our own farms.

One could also be asked to clear the weeds growing in someone's back yard in exchange for some money.

At other times my peers and I went on expeditions to hunt animals such as squirrels, Gambian pouched rats, grasscutters, etc. Sometimes we returned from a whole day's expedition empty-handed. At other times luck smiled on us, and we returned with our hunting sack filled with various kinds of game. On such occasions, we gave part of our catch to our parents and sold the rest. The money we obtained was shared equally among ourselves.

--51--
THE TRAGIC END OF 'POOR NO FRIEND'

MANY HOUSEHOLDS IN THE VILLAGE KEPT DOGS. It was common practice for residents to give their dogs names that reflected their thinking on various aspects of this life, be it religious, social, financial or romantic—*Nyame Bekyere* (God will direct affairs and provide for one's needs); *Ehia wo a enwu* (Do not allow poverty and want to lead you to commit suicide); *Poor No Friend* etc.

We kept various dogs at various stages of my life at Mpintimpi. It was not just the love for them that led us to keep them; we did so mainly because we needed them for our hunting expeditions.

One did not necessarily have to possess one's own dog to go hunting with one. Instead, one could approach one's neighbours or friends to beg for the use of their dog. One could easily get the neighbour to agree to such a request. Getting a dog to accompany a strange person could pose a real problem, of course. In our small village, however, not only were the human inhabitants conversant with one another, but intelligent animals like dogs normally got used to members of the community.

The practice was to offer a dog directly responsible for catching a prey the head of the catch to enjoy. Regardless of whether a dog was responsible for a catch or not, it was sure to receive the intestines of most prey.

Even as I write, the tragic circumstances that led to the death of *Poor No Friend* have sprung to memory. It occurred during one of our hunting expeditions, just as we were in hot pursuit of a grasscutter. As often happened in such situations, we struggled to keep pace with the prey and the dog pursuing it. Suddenly our brave dog began to bark loudly. We wondered what was the matter with him.

Thinking it had got at the prey, we rushed to the scene but soon the barks turned into yelps of agony.. The answer came quickly! As we were a distance of about ten metres away, we realised a huge python had coiled around him, mercilessly suffocating the helpless dog to death.

There was little we could do to help him, other than stand and watch helplessly as our beloved *Poor No Friend* was crushed to death by the awful beast.

--52--
THE VOCIFEROUS WIVES AND THE AGING FOOTBALLERS

FOOTBALL is the most popular sport in Ghana. The situation was no different at the time I was growing up. Whenever time permitted us, my peers and I got together to play our favourite game. We made use of any large open space we could find.

When one of us wished to play football, all he did was to go from house to house looking for any of his peers who were ready to join him.

We rarely possessed proper balls. Instead, we made use of oranges. We went round inspecting the orange trees growing within and also along the fringes of the village. Often we discovered fruits that had attained sizes suitable for the purpose—they should not be too small to be kicked around, nor too ripe in order to withstand the pressure of kicking it for a while.

Occasionally some of our relatives living in the large towns paid a visit to the village and presented us with a plastic ball. One can imagine our joy on such occasions! When we were fortunate, the plastic balls could last for several weeks if not months before they got torn apart.

On other occasions luck was not on our side, however; hardly had we got hold of the new ball than it was punctured by a sharp object—a piece of broken glass, a needle, the thorn of a shrub or plant growing along the edges of the playground, etc. When that happened we were left with no choice but to return to our oranges and hope for the next opportunity in the distant future when someone might present us with yet another proper ball.

We had a relatively large open space bordering the fringes of our home. This, combined with the fact that mother had blessed our village with several boys who were all keen to play football at the least opportunity, made our compound a popular meeting place for boys in the community who were keen to enjoy a game of football.

In the course of time, the adults in the community formed their own football club. Over a long period they struggled to agree on a name for the club. In the end they settled on 'Mpintimpi Eleven'!

I still clearly remember the day the adult football team gathered together on a patch of dense bush on the fringes of the village to develop their own football pitch. Needless to say, their resources did not permit them to engage a firm that specialised in landscape design. Instead, they relied on their own manual labour and 'know-how' to get the job done.

To begin with, with the help of machetes, they cleared the thick bush encroaching on the land. Next, they felled whatever trees that were in the way. This was accomplished either with the help of machetes or axes.

The most tedious part of the undertaking involved uprooting the stumps of the trees they had already axed. With no machines to help them, they had to make use of instruments such as axes and pickaxes to cut and dig down around the tree stumps in order finally to uproot them.

Through a painstaking and lengthy process of uprooting grass from various locations and replanting it on the field, they managed in time to cover the whole pitch with grass.

The goalposts were not made of metal, but wood, hard tropical wood that was resilient enough to withstand the elements for a considerable period of time without becoming rotten.

Through their own sweat, Mpintimpi Eleven eventually acquired a decent football pitch. That was as far as they could go, however. Though there was constant talk of acquiring a set of jerseys as well as a set of football boots for the whole team, financial constraints prevented them from realising their goal. In the end they left it to each player to wear whatever outfit he could afford. A few managed to play with a pair of canvas shoes; the majority however relied on their 'God-given boots'.

One thing that Mpintimpi Eleven was not lacking in was ambition. Although a football club of a small village, they did not shun from organising matches with neighbouring towns like Afosu and Akuase, each about five times(if not more) the size of our village.

Such friendly matches were played on a home and away basis, with the team first to play home travelling two weeks later to the other for the return match. Football, football! Considerable tension and excitement surrounded such meetings. When the match finally got underway, the emotions on both sides could soar to the high heavens. Under such a charged atmosphere any decision from the referee that led the other team or their fans to feel cheated could precipitate an explosive situation.

In rare instances, what was dubbed a friendly match could lead to an exchange of blows, not only on the pitch, but also among the rival supporters! When that happened, the team that hosted the match refused to travel for the return match out of fear of possible reprisals.

Mpintimpi Eleven did not always play with outsiders; on some occasions they organised matches among their own members. The manner in which they formed teams to play among themselves was not devoid of ingenuity. Sometimes it was 'Amanfa versus Amanfa', the Twi word *Amanfa* meaning literally 'one half of the town'. As I mentioned on a previous occasion, a trunk road goes through the village dividing it into almost two equal halves. In Amanfa versus Amanfa, residents on one side of the road were pitted against those on the other side.

On other occasions, the contest was between Asigyafo and Awarefo where the Twi word *osigyani* (plural *asigyafo*) stands for 'an unmarried person' and *owareni* (plural *awarefo*) means 'a married person'. A considerable degree of pre- and post-match excitement accompanied meetings involving the two groups. Whereas the team of the bachelors was comprised mostly of teenagers and young adults bursting with vitality, their counterparts were in the main men aged thirty and over.

By virtue of the constitution of the teams, one would usually expect the bachelors to come out as winners. That was not always the case, however. On a few occasions, the team of married players, cheered on by their vociferous wives, defied the odds and clinched victory over their more agile opponents.

I have always been a keen adherent of the game of football. Prior to the onset of the problem with my left ankle, I played in any position my team assigned me. Due to the problem with my left ankle, however, my football involvement was restricted to goalkeeping.

Later I assumed the role of referee, both for the youth as well as the adult team. Whether I managed always to execute my office judiciously without fear or favour of players or their managers is left to those who experienced my refereeing activities to judge.

--53--
FIRST THE SWEAT THEN THE BALLS

AN ACCOUNT OF MY LIFE at Mpintimpi will not, in my opinion, be complete if I fail to dedicate some lines to the preparation of *fufu*, our main evening meal. Fufu indeed is the main meal of the majority of Ghanaians as well as residents in several parts of west Africa. Though it can be enjoyed at any time of day, it is usually eaten as the last meal of the day.

A complete stranger to our locality, for example a tourist visiting from the US or Europe, would, in the evening, around 5 pm, wonder what for God's sake was behind the rhythmic *p-u-u-m! p-u-u-m!! p-u-u-m!!!* sound emanating from almost every home in the little settlement. The answer would be that it was the time of day that almost all households in the settlement would be pounding fufu.

A meal of fufu has two main components: the fufu balls and the soup to go with it. The ingredients that are pounded into fufu balls can vary depending on the choice of the person involved. At Mpintimpi we usually prepared our balls by pounding boiled cassava together with either plantain or cocoyam. Elsewhere in the country, only yam or cassava or a combination of both may be used.

Fufu is pounded in a wooden mortar using a wooden pestle. Pounding is done by one or more persons at the same time (for practical reasons it is unusual for more than three 'pounders' to do so at the same time) who assume a semi-circular standing position around the mortar. Another person takes a seat beside the mortar, facing the pounders.

The process begins when the person sitting beside the mortar begins to place, one after the other, cooked chunks of plantain or cassava or cocoyam, as the case may be, into the mortar. As the 'driver' (as we refer to the person sitting) does so, the pounder(s) pound the pieces of food to crush them.

It is the duty of the driver to ensure the crushed pieces of food do not fall from the mortar to the ground. After the last chunk of food has been crushed, the driver turns the crushed food until the dough sticks together and forms a smooth ball. The job of the driver is not without risks. Though it rarely happens, the act of turning the crushed food around in the mortar at the same time that the pounders are busy at work could result in one or more fingers being struck by a pestle.

When I was growing up, I initially took part in the laborious process of pounding. As a result of the problem with my left ankle, for a while I was exempt from the arduous task. Eventually, I learnt to be a driver. In time I gained considerable experience in the 'trade'. Even then, I got one or more fingers hit on a few occasions. Fortunately, in all instances I escaped with only a bruise.

The unique thing about fufu is that one does not have to chew it; instead, one has to 'cut' a small lump with the fingers, dip the piece into the soup, place it on the tongue and swallow it. For a stranger attempting to enjoy fufu for the first time, this may be challenging, but with some practice one can master the ritual.

The pounders and driver of fufu must work in harmony to ensure an optimal outcome of their efforts. Mother used to tell us the story of a married couple who, at one stage in their relationship, were not on talking terms with each other, though they shared the same roof. The woman, as usual, set about preparing an evening meal of fufu. Eventually, she assembled all the ingredients required and took her seat near the mortar without saying a word to her husband. He understood the signal, picked up the pestle and took his position. His wife then began placing the ingredients into the mortar. Soon the pounding began.

Though communication is important to ensure progress, still neither of the two was prepared to break the silence. The man continued pounding the crushed foodstuff until he was convinced it was ready to be served. At that stage he ceased pounding. The wife understood the signal, removed the balls from the mortar and served the meal into a single dish. Still not speaking to each other, both of them set about to enjoy the delicious meal. Mother could not tell how long the situation persisted in the marriage.

At one stage when I was growing up, rumours began to spread to the effect that engineers at the University of Science and Technology in Kumasi, Ghana's second largest city, had come up with a device that could be used to pound fufu.

Mother's reaction on hearing this is still fresh in my memory.

"Fufu pounded by a machine?" she burst out. "God forbid!"

"What is wrong with that?" one of us wanted to know.

"It will not taste like the original fufu!"

"Why not? The same ingredients will be used. The only difference is that the machine does the pounding instead of a human being!"

"You will never get me to eat that kind of fufu! Since time immemorial we have pounded our fufu! That is what I will continue to do so long as I have breath."

Mother was not alone in her attitude. Indeed, for many persons, especially those of her generation, fufu is only fufu if it is prepared in the traditional way, never mind if the process of pounding is a laborious, time-consuming exercise, not achieved without the shedding of considerable sweat.

As I write this, powdered components of the popular dish have become available on the market. In Ghana it is used mainly by the middle and upper class of society who, apart from not having the time to invest preparing fufu in the traditional way, have the means to purchase it on a regular basis. (It is more expensive than the traditional method, as might be expected.)

How would mother, who passed away in July 1994, react to fufu balls being obtained not through pounding, but by stirring powdered ingredients in hot water, I wonder?

--54--
DOUBLE TRAGEDY AROUND THE BATHROOM

THE FIRST THING we did on waking up was to wash our face and clean our teeth. We did not make use of toothbrushes or toothpaste. We resorted instead to the chewing stick and chewing brush. Several species of trees and shrubs are used as chewing sticks in Ghana. At Mpintimpi, the most popular chewing sticks are *tweapea* and *nsorkodua*, which belong to the Garcinia species of plants. (Such plants are noted for their chemical properties that help to prevent tooth decay and remove bad mouth odour.)

The process of cleaning the teeth with a chewing stick involves chewing one end of the stick into a brush or tuft and using it to clean the teeth the way one would use a toothbrush. After a while, the tuft is consumed; one has to chew on the stick another time to replace the tuft. The time one spends cleaning the teeth with a stick varies, and depends on how much time one has at one's disposal.

Children too small to chew on the stick usually cleaned their teeth by means of a brush obtained by beating the skin of the plantain fruit together with charcoal.

If it was extremely difficult to obtain proper medical care in the village, one can imagine the situation when it came to finding a dentist. How many residents of the village lived their whole lives without ever visiting a dentist!?

Needless to say, I never visited the dentist throughout my childhood days. My first confrontation with the 'tooth doctor' came when I was about 17 years old. I had gone to have a shower at the boarding school when I slipped and fell on my face, in the process breaking half of one of my front teeth. The root was still strong so the dentist left it untouched and prescribed only painkillers.

Poor me! Several years later, when I was residing at the campus of the University in Ghana at Legon, in Accra, I slipped, fell and broke half of another front tooth! The reader can only wonder what I was I doing at that time! Again, it had to do with the bathroom, though this time I was not yet in the bathroom but heading towards it when I slipped! That precipitated my second confrontation with the tooth doctor.

I cannot therefore assign blame to the lifestyle I was exposed to at Mpintimpi for the dental problems that developed later in my life. Rarely was I exposed to sweets. Though we produced cocoa beans, from which chocolate and other sweets are produced, hardly anyone living in our village had any idea what chocolate tasted like. It was once in a blue moon, when some of our relatives living in the towns came by for a visit, that they presented us with a few pieces of toffee, cakes, chewing gum, etc.

--55--
A PECULIAR METHOD OF BATTERY-CHARGING

THOUGH THE OVERWHELMING MAJORITY of the population of Mpintimpi was illiterate, one could sense a general yearning amongst them for information concerning events in the country. The villagers—at least the few who could afford them—relied mainly on battery-powered transistor radios as their main source of information.

At that time, the state-controlled Ghana Broadcasting Corporation, GBC for short, was the main source of information not only for residents of the village but also for many parts of the rural areas. Initially, GBC boasted only two channels, GBC 1 which targeted the local population, and GBC External, which, as the name suggests, was meant for listeners beyond the borders of the country. In the course of time GBC 2, also known as GBC Commercial (to reflect the fact that it carried commercials) was also introduced.

Prior to the advent of GBC 2, GBC 1 broadcast in English as well as in the major languages of the country—Twi, Ga, Ewe, Hausa, Dagbani and Nzema. With the introduction of GBC 2, GBC 1 ceased to broadcast in English. The only exception was when it joined GBC2 on the top of certain hours to carry the news bulletin in English.

Father possessed his own transistor radio. He was a keen listener of the radio, not only to follow the events going on in Ghana and beyond, but also to listen to music, in particular traditional highlife music. That was a source of tension between him and his 'young academics' who also wanted to use the only radio of the family to inform and entertain themselves. As I mentioned earlier, he lived in his extended family home whereas we lived with mother in the house he built for us.

Still, from time to time, he lent out the wireless set to us. He was reluctant to do so on Sundays, however, the day on which matches of the national football league were played. Father loved football and was keen to follow the radio commentary, especially when it involved matches of Kumasi Asante Kotoko, the favourite team of the whole family.

It was for this very reason that his children also yearned to have access to his wireless set on Sundays! One would imagine we could resolve the matter by gathering round the wireless set with him to listen to the commentary together—that on the surface would appear to be a good solution. There was a hitch, however. Father, who had no knowledge of the English language, understandably preferred to follow the events in Twi on GBC 1.

Well, we might as well have done so with him. The problem however was that GBC 1 did not broadcast only in the Twi language but, as previously mentioned, in several other languages most of which were like Latin to us. To be fair to all sides, the football commentary on GBC 1 switched from one language to the other.

Even when the commentary switched over from Twi to another language, the head of the family was reluctant to allow us to tune in to GBC 2. He was probably acting on the basis of his past experience, for he knew that once he allowed us to do so, it would be difficult to persuade us to return to GBC 1!

Though he loved listening to his radio, there were occasions when circumstances beyond his control forced him, if only temporarily, to do without his favourite source of information and entertainment.

I have stressed on several occasions that money was generally difficult to come by at Mpintimpi. Father's wireless set required six alkaline size D batteries. On several occasions, the batteries ran down at the very time when he did not have the means to replace them. When that happened he sought in his own way to recharge them by removing them from the 'talking machine' and placing them upright on the bare cement floor for several hours. Usually, after they had been exposed to the comparatively cool surface of the cement floor for a while, the batteries 'recharged'.

Please do not ask me the mechanism behind this. The fact remains that the batteries did regain some strength, permitting him to continue listening to his programmes, for a while at least. In due course, however, hearing became so difficult for him that he reserved the energy left in the batteries for listening to what to him was the most important programme of the day, namely the ten-minute Twi news bulletin that was broadcast daily at 6:15 pm.

A time finally arrived when the batteries did not allow themselves to be recharged in the innovative manner described above. Soon the wireless set gave up its spirit and remained still.

Father would then wait until a good opportunity came by, when his resources permitted him to replace the batteries. Often he did not manage to replace all six at the same time. Instead he did so in 'instalments'—he purchased, for example, three new ones which together with the 'dying or already dead ones' managed to bring the wireless set back to life, temporarily, at least.

--56--
THOSE WHO SHARE THEIR LAST PINS WITH THEIR NEIGHBOURS

AT MPINTIMPI, the inhabitants acquired the habit of sharing, not as a luxury, but rather as a necessity—yes, as a means of survival. For impoverished as we were, hardly any one of us could have mastered the challenges of day-to-day life on his or her own. In the end, residents approached each other for help in almost every aspect of life—from the trivial to the substantial.

In the following passage, I will outline some of the ways each individual depended on another in the community.

When we returned home in the late afternoon from work on our fields, we needed to restart the fire in our kitchen. After we had gathered firewood in a makeshift clay stove, mother sent one of us on an errand to the neighbouring homes to collect fire to help start our own fire. We moved from house to house in the neighbourhood until we came to a home where their fire was already burning. No longer had we started our fire than others also came to us to collect some of our fire to help them start their fire.

We also shared food, cooked or uncooked, with our neighbours.

Sharing was not restricted to foodstuffs and burning coals; it also extended to several aspects of everyday life.

Residents, for example, approached their neighbours to borrow pieces of java clothes, sandals, head kerchiefs, belts, etc., to wear either on normal days or on occasions of important social gatherings such as funerals, weddings, traditional festivals, etc.

--57--
FOR CREDIT COME TOMORROW

THE WIDESPREAD POVERTY that prevailed in Mpintimpi affected the way and manner business was conducted. During the time I was growing up there, mother, from time to time engaged in petty trading to supplement our income. The items we bought and sold included canned fish (mainly sardines and mackerel), packets of safety matches, pens, pencils, exercise books, cooking oil and table salt. In an interval of about eight weeks, mother travelled to Nkawkaw and bought small amounts of the items listed for further resale in the little settlement.

During the years when the yield of food crops from our farm was reasonably substantial, mother also used to operate what is known locally as a 'chop bar' (a small restaurant). In a small village like ours the tendency was to operate the 'chop bar' in the home setting. All that the proprietor need do was to acquire a couple of chairs, dining tables, as well as about a dozen plates, soup bowls and ordinary drinking cups. One could well do without items like spoons, forks and knives, for the large proportion of customers who went there to eat preferred to eat with their fingers.

It was a bone-breaking affair, the task of getting the meals ready to be served to our customers. Although we did our best to assist her, mother did the greater part of the work herself.

The first customers began arriving as early as six in the morning. Those who showed up at that time of day were in the main farmers who wanted to break their fast early to get to their farms in good time.

After all the effort we invested to get the products to the customer—be it a hot breakfast, the tins of canned sardines, or boxes of safety matches—we expected them to show their appreciation by offering ready cash in return for the goods. In practice this proved to be wishful thinking on our part! Usually, after we handed our customers the products and demanded payment, many of them came up with statements like these:

"I do not have any money on me today. Just give me one week. By then some of the crops on my farm will be ripe for harvesting."

If we thought that individual was the only person who hoped to purchase on credit that day, we would soon realise that was not the case. Indeed, the next, and the next, *and* still the next customer might all come up with their stories and plead with us to allow them to buy on credit.

A time eventually came when our cup of patience drained away, when the practice of selling on credit was having an adverse effect on our trade returns. At that juncture, one of us would look out for a wooden slate or a cardboard and write boldly one of the following inscriptions:

FOR CREDIT COME TOMORROW
PAY AS YOU BUY
NO MONEY, NO EXCHANGE OF GOODS

We positioned the sign strategically so that it was plainly visible to anyone seeking to buy from us. By word of mouth and well in advance we informed customers who had not been able to read and digest the newly introduced trade guidelines of the strictly cash basis for acquiring the products we were selling.

Our efforts did not yield the desired results, for all of a sudden we began to lose a considerable number of our customers. When we questioned some of them to find out why they no longer gave us their custom, they replied that while understanding our motives for insisting on immediate payment, their inability to meet our demands left them with no choice but to stay away.

The fact that they were not buying from us did not mean they had to do without the products they were desirous to acquire, however. After all, ours was not the only place in the village from which they could acquire the goods they sought. Sooner rather than later, we were forced to reverse our set rules of business engagement rather than find ourselves squeezed out of business.

From time to time mother would send some of her children on rounds through the village to call on our debtors and urge them to pay what they owed us. Armed with our little credit notebooks, we called on them to demand payment.

Our experience on such rounds was often disheartening, to put it mildly. When we were several metres away from the home of some of them, we could spot them, for example, seated under the shade at one corner of the compound, cuddling a baby or occupied doing something else. As we drew nearer, we would realise to our surprise that the individual we had, a few seconds earlier, seen with our own naked eyes had evaporated into thin air! When we inquired from the children there about the whereabouts of their mothers or fathers or both, we were confronted with statements like:

- "He/she is yet to return from work on the farm!"
- "He/she has left for the riverside to fetch water!"
- "He/she is sick in bed and not in a position to be talked to at the moment!"

Those debtors one was fortunate to meet at home sent us away with stories like:

- "Madam A has just bought the squirrel I brought home on a hunting trip. She has promised to make payment this evening. You should come again tomorrow."
- "My husband is yet to return from work on the fields. You might try again around the same time tomorrow."
- "The clerk of the CMB has left for Nkawkaw to collect money to pay for the cocoa beans he bought from us. Try again tomorrow or the day after."

We counted ourselves lucky when we got a debtor to make outright payment on a first call. Usually we reckoned with a minimum of three calls per debtor before we could come by the monies due to us.

I must admit we did not only offer others credit; often we also bought from others on credit!

Not only was it a widespread habit to buy and sell goods on credit in the village; those who rented out their rooms to the few strangers in our midst could similarly not always count on the prompt payment of the rent due. In some instances the arrears could pile up to as much as six months' rent. What could the property owners do but resort to persuasion and also count on the goodwill of their tenants to make payment?

--58--
UNCONVENTIONAL SAVING'S BANKS AND THUMB-PRINTED AGREEMENTS

IN A SOCIETY where the overwhelming majority of residents ride on bicycles, one might still come across a few who manage to ride on motorbikes.

The same could be said of the inhabitants of our little community. A handful of them, while not fulfilling the criteria to be described as well-to-do in a place like Accra, the national capital, were sufficiently well-off to be able to put some money aside—albeit not considerable amounts—which they lent to other inhabitants who approached them for help.

The nearest available bank was at Nkawkaw, which, as I mentioned earlier, was several kilometres away. Hardly anyone in the village made use of their services. One might want to know where such 'well-to-do's' of the community kept their surplus money. Several wild rumours made their rounds concerning the matter. Some spoke of some individuals digging holes near landmark objects on their farms and concealing their money, wrapped tightly in plastic bags to prevent the elements from destroying them.

Some of the wild stories went on to say that death took some of those individuals by surprise, leaving them no time to notify their relatives about their hidden wealth. Others were said to have managed, just at the very last seconds of their struggle with the inevitable outcome of their mortality, to pass their secret on to family members.

Usually the need to borrow money arose when someone fell seriously ill and needed to be taken to hospital. Initially, extended family members of the person thus affected pooled their resources. Sometimes, all the resources of fathers, mothers, uncles, nieces, aunties, etc., were pooled together and yet remained insufficient. In such a situation, they consulted residents of the settlement generally regarded as being well-to-do for help. There were instances, though, when no one in the settlement could help. If that happened, family members looked beyond the borders of the village—for example Afosu and Nyafoman—for the needed help.

Despite their meagre resources, my parents made the bold decision to send their second child, Ransford, after he gained admission, to Oda Secondary School, a boarding school at the district capital. Though they themselves did not get the opportunity to attend school, they decided not to allow the golden opportunity to slip by for their son.

Over the next five years their decision brought them into considerable financial difficulty, for though tuition was free, boarding and lodging were not. On several occasions, Ransford was sent home to collect boarding fees that were in arrears. If only they could find someone who could lend them the needed amount pending the arrival of the cocoa season!

Father would approach someone he considered likely to be in a position to help and revealed the details of his precarious financial situation only to be told in the end: "My good friend, how I wish I could help you! Unfortunately, my shoe is also pressing. I am also patiently awaiting the arrival of the cocoa season!"

Still, after a long search, my parents usually managed to find someone who was able to lend them all or part of the sum involved. Repayment was always with interest, which was set arbitrarily by the lender.

On a few occasions one had to pledge one's property, usually a cocoa farm over a specified period of years in exchange for the loan. During the whole period of the pledge the entire yield from the portion of farm in question went to the lender.

Some lenders were considerate and entrusted the piece of land to the borrower for care-taking. In that instance, the borrower received part of the yield, usually one-third, as compensation. There were instances, however, when the lender decided either to take care of the land themselves or to entrust it to a third party to do so.

If the piece of land happened to be the only one of its kind that the borrower possessed, pledging it for a year or two, or even for longer, could have dire financial consequences not only for themselves, but also for their dependants.

Though a simple society, when it came to matters of money, the principle 'trust but verify' held sway. In keeping with that thinking, a formal loan agreement was written down on paper, not before lawyers, but before witnesses from the community.

The task of writing down such agreements on paper fell to the few 'academics' of the settlement. Initially my senior brothers, especially Ransford, did the loan agreements, involving not only father, but also other members of the community at large.

Later, the composer of these lines was also called upon, from time to time, to perform the task.

Since it usually involved illiterates, the task of translating the deed of agreement to both parties and their witnesses (one from each side) fell also to the writer. The agreement was finally sealed with the right thumbprint of lender, borrower and a witness for each party. Each of them was expected to set the print of the thumb beneath their respective name. Needless to say, the duty usually fell to the 'secretary' to guide each respective thumb to the corresponding name.

--59--
"THEY SAY I HAVE TB!"

ONE DAY WE HAD JUST RETURNED HOME from work on the farm and were busily preparing our evening meal when we spotted a middle-aged man, about fifty years old, approaching our home from the centre of the village. Mother soon recognised the stranger and began shouting:

"O-n-i o-o-o-h!"(Here he comes!) at the top of her voice.

"Who is that?" one of us wanted to know.

"It is your uncle; one of my brothers", she replied.

We were surprised to hear mother speak about her brother! We were aware she had two elderly sisters living in Amantia, her hometown. That she still had a living brother was something that we were hearing for the first time.

"Hurry up children, go and help your uncle with his luggage!" she instructed us. Without asking any more questions, one of us hurried to the stranger, collected his bag from his hands, and carried it the few remaining metres to our home.

As it turned out, our late visitor was a distant relation of mother's. That she chose to refer to him as a brother may surprise the reader who is not familiar with our local setting. As I mentioned earlier, as far as traditional African culture is concerned, any distant relation can be described as one's 'brother' or 'sister', as the case may be.

Mother warmly welcomed the unannounced visitor to our home. Custom has it that after a person visiting one's home has been offered a seat, he or she is given water to quench their thirst. After they have drunk some water and relaxed for a while, they are then formally asked by the host to explain the reason for their visit, even if the reason is already known by the host.

In keeping with this tradition, mother, after offering him a seat and some water, inquired from her visiting relation the reason for his visit.

"I have not been well for a while", he began. "As usual, I tried traditional medicine with the hope of regaining my health. Unfortunately that did not help. In the end, with the help of other members of the extended family, I managed to raise enough funds to enable me to attend hospital. I could have attended the hospital at Akim Oda. As you are aware, that is nearer to Amantia. I was however told by some members of our family that Nkawkaw is better suited for my condition. "I left for the hospital very early today with the hope of being able to return home after seeing the doctor.

"I was seen by the doctor early in the day. Unfortunately, when I got to the 'lorry park' there was no vehicle travelling as far as Amantia. Eventually I found one heading for Afosu. Just then it occurred to me that one of my own was living at Mpintimpi, which the vehicle would pass on its way to Afosu. I said to myself: 'Why not spend the night with her rather than hang around at Nkawkaw? After all, you do not have enough money to stay at a hotel.'

"So I joined the vehicle. As you are aware, I have never been here before. I was certain though that I would not have any difficulty finding you. That turned out to be the case, for the first person I spoke to on alighting from the vehicle pointed straight to your home. So I am here to spend the night and resume my journey first thing tomorrow."

"No problem", mother replied. "You are welcome in our home." She then turned to us: "Children, carry your uncle's bag into your room. He will sleep there tonight; you will sleep with us."

Initially uncle did not reveal to us what had led him to the doctors. It did not take long, however, for us to realise something was seriously wrong with him, for no sooner had he settled down than he began to cough, almost unceasingly. He coughed so loudly that my young mind began to think his chest would burst open.

If his coughing was a source of concern to us, what soon followed sent shockwaves through our spines—uncle did not cough out ordinary phlegm but blood, pure red blood!

"What is the matter with you, Yaw!?" mother inquired, terrified.
"They say I have TB!"
"TB?"
"Yes."
"That is serious!"
"They have given me medicine to take home. They have asked me to report back after some days if there is no improvement."

Although mother did not know the details concerning TB, she was aware it was a serious disease. Was she aware he could pass it on to us? I am not sure she was. Even if she did know, the idea would never have occurred to her to show our visitor the door once he was settled with us.

To treat a relation, yes a member of the extended family in that manner, especially at that hour of the day, was out of the question. Indeed, had she refused to allow him to stay, how would other members of the family have reacted on hearing the news? They would probably have described mother as self-centred and cold-hearted, one who refused to show compassion to a member of the family, yes, one of hers, at the very moment when he needed her help.

Uncle continued to cough and spit out blood for the most part of the night. After breakfast the next morning, he joined a vehicle to continue his homeward journey. About three months after his visit, word reached us that he had passed away. As tradition required, mother left for Amantia to bid a final farewell to one of her own.

--60--
APOLLO 11 WREAKS HAVOC ON THE STREETS OF TINY MPINTIMPI

IN THE MIDDLE OF 1969 a highly contagious eye disease began to afflict not only residents of the little village but also the population of Ghana as a whole. Reports even spoke of the disease having spread to other countries in west Africa. Though several years ago, I recall the typical symptoms of the disease—a red, painful and itchy eye. The moment an individual in a household was afflicted, it was just a matter of days if not hours before it spread to the other inhabitants.

Readers might recall that the Apollo 11 mission landed on the moon on 20th July 1969. The eye disease, coming hard on the heels, as it were, of the time of the Apollo 11 landing on the moon led to rumours spreading throughout Ghana (and probably beyond) to the effect that the crew of that historic mission brought the disease back with them on their return from the moon!

Subsequently, the eye disease, which was later christened *acute hemorrhagic conjunctivitis*, AHC for short, by the medical experts and said to be caused by the AHC virus, came to be known as 'Apollo 11'! Almost every resident of our village fell victim to what to us was a mysterious eye disease. Fortunately, the disease vanished the way it came, without leaving lasting scars on its victims.

The eye infection coinciding with the Apollo 11 mission helped to raise the awareness of the villagers of the mission and at the same time help nurture all kinds of rumours and speculations within the predominantly illiterate population as to the motive behind the mission.

"The Americans have plans to settle on the moon in future!" someone claimed.

"The Americans have plans to install a bomb on the moon from where they can hit the Russians!" another rumour had it.

Mother contributed to the debate in her own way.

"Who can take me to those responsible for the mission to the moon?" she began.

"What do you want from them?" one of her children inquired.

"I want to discuss one or two issues with them!"

"What, then?"

"I want to tell them to their face my own opinion of their undertaking."

"What will you tell them?"

"It will be plain speaking, very plain speaking. I will begin like this: 'Ladies and gentlemen, may I have your attention? I hail from a very little village with the difficult to pronounce name, Mpintimpi. In our village, our children die from want of good drinking water. We have no hospital near us. Worse still, the road linking us to the distant hospital is in such a bad state, the sick are so shaken in the vehicles transporting them, some die before they get there. Time will not allow me to list all our woes. The village dwellers have learnt that you are extremely wealthy. Your wealth has enabled you to venture to the moon. Could you please be merciful to us, honourable ladies and gentlemen, and help us develop our village? Please do something for us before we die in our poverty.'"

"No one will listen to you, mother! They will tell you that matters in regard to the development of your village do not fall within their sphere of responsibility. You would be better advised to bring your needs before the Government in Accra than waste money, time and energy to travel the distance to America to bother them with your problems."

"I would refuse to allow them to send me away with such arguments. No, never!"

"What else could you do?"

"'Wait a moment, ladies and gentlemen', I would hit back, 'we share the same planet, we breathe the same air, we all suffer when the vehicles stuffing your streets pollute the atmosphere. Even more recently all the residents of my village have been suffering as a result of your mission to the moon. Look at my eyes, ladies and gentlemen! You notice how red they have turned? I am suffering from the 'Apollo 11' eye disease your people brought back with them from the moon!'"

They would say "How can you prove, old woman, that our mission has anything, directly or indirectly, to do with your eye disease?"

"Ah, you children of today! Never since the time of our forefathers has there been such an outbreak in our peaceful village. Take it from me, your people brought it with them!"

--61--
TABLE SALT FOR A VOTE CAST

IN 1966 THE MILITARY OVERTHREW the regime of Dr Kwame Nkrumah; he had ruled Ghana since independence in 1957. Though I was too young to understand anything, one thing I do recall was the jubilation that took place on the streets of our little village during the several days that followed the event. As we learnt from the radio, the expression of joy displayed in the village was not restricted to our small community but was also observed in several parts of the country.

Three years after the *coup d'etat*, the military Government called for a general election in preparation for a handover of power to a civilian administration. The general election took place on 29th August 1969.

The election was preceded by several weeks of an election campaign. On a regular basis, the campaign trail of one of the several parties came to a stop at our little village, their vehicles clad in the colours of their various parties, and adorned by bold pictures of the respective candidates.

My peers and I were not so much interested in the message they carried as the fanfare that accompanied their visit. "*Eye Pro, Eye Sure!*" (It is pro, it is sure!) the Progress Party (PP) people chanted in their megaphones.

Hardly had the dust following on the trails of the PP begun to settle than the campaigning vehicles of the National Alliance of Liberals (NAL) also arrived.

Though other small parties were involved in the campaign, the PP and the NAL were the main contenders.

The majority of residents supported the PP, though quite a reasonable proportion supported the second leading party.

In the afternoons, when they met under the palm wine tapper's hut, adherents of the various parties argued it out as to which party was best suited to govern the country. The arguments were on the whole peaceful. I cannot recall a time when it turned violent, leading, for example, to physical confrontation.

In the end the PP won the national election, and their leading candidate, Dr Busia, became Prime Minister. The PP not only won the national election, their parliamentary candidate for our constituency did so as well. Eventually he toured the constituency to express his thanks to the voters. On a stop in our village, he handed the Chief several bags of salt for further distribution to the residents.

Mother was furious on hearing the news.

"Where can I find him?"

"Why?"

"I want to have a chat with him!"

"Why? What would you tell him?"

"I will tell him to his face that I did not vote for him for the sake of common table salt! I have been buying my salt all along. I am sure with God's help I will be able to continue doing so." She shook her head. "No—I voted for him for something else—for an improvement in our living conditions. We need amenities such as good drinking water, a clinic, good roads. My goodness! What do these politicians think of us villagers? Stupid citizens whose votes they can purchase with paltry items like table salt?"

Barely twenty-seven months after the peaceful handover, the military staged yet another coup to overthrow the elected Government.

Unlike the Nkrumah regime, they accused the Busia regime not with dictatorial tendencies but rather for the rising cost of living in the country.

The same people who went out on the main street of the village in 1966 to celebrate the overthrow of Dr Nkrumah's administration, returned again to express their joy at the forceful overthrow of the Busia Government!

Residents of Mpintimpi, and the country at large, have in the meantime learnt their lessons in the areas of political culture, democracy, freedom of speech, civil liberties, etc., since multiparty democracy has become well established in the country. Since 1992, the country has held several generally peaceful elections leading to the smooth transfer of power from one administration to the other.

It was not by accident that in July 2009, President Obama chose Ghana, the small country on the west African coast, to deliver a political speech to the whole of Africa.

--62--
THE YOUNG TRAVELLER WHO MISSED HIS MOTHER'S KITCHEN

AS I MENTIONED at the beginning of my narration, at the time I was big enough to attend school there was no school in our village, and so we were forced to walk to school in Nyafoman. Four years after starting school the local authorities decided to open a primary school in the village. It was too late for us, though, for it admitted only Year 1 pupils.

One of the first teachers to be posted to Mpintimpi Local Authority Primary School, as the school was christened, was Teacher Ansah. He hailed from Twereso, a large town about eighty kilometres from Mpintimpi, not far from Akim Oda, the district capital.

As might be expected, the villagers welcomed with open arms the learned individual, who was there to impart his knowledge to their children.

Teacher Ansah rented a room in father's extended family home. Father and mother showed him kindness, treating him as one of their children.

In the course of time the well-respected resident of the little community developed a particular liking for me. Why that was so is a fact that baffled me.

In the first place, I was not a pupil of his school. Besides that, there were several other kids in the village he could have befriended.

One evening, a few days before schools closed for the Christmas holiday, he approached father and began:

"I would like to take my little friend along with me for the Christmas holidays!"

"Really?" father replied, rather taken aback.

"Yes! I would like to show him to my parents and the rest of the family."

"I do not have anything against it. I will pass the message on to his mother and himself to know what they think about your proposal."

Mother was initially sceptical, but when she noticed how delighted I was at the idea, she dropped her reservations. She was only concerned that I might miss home, since I had until then never travelled away from home on my own.

I could hardly wait for the day to arrive. For a start I scarcely ever got the opportunity to travel on a vehicle! Mother occasionally took us on a visit to Amantia, her hometown. That was once in a blue moon though—at best once in two years. As I mentioned at the outset, occasionally some drivers gave us a lift on our way to or from school—but that was also very seldom indeed. Of course I was excited about the chance to explore the unknown.

The eagerly awaited day finally arrived. Together with my big friend we boarded a vehicle that took us safely to our destination.

I was warmly welcomed by his family. Soon I was mingling with the family members of my age group. On the street, they introduced me to their peers, who in turn greeted me warmly, extending the invitation to me to join them in a game of football whenever I could.

Mother knew what she was talking about! A few days after the arrival of the 'village boy' in town, I began to feel homesick—not that I was not accepted by my hosts. No, the reason that led me to miss my small village lay somewhere else—and had more to do with the demands of my stomach than neglect by those I was visiting.

The food specialist might classify the meals mother provided her children as being unbalanced or one-sided. Based on my present knowledge, I will not dispute that assertion. Of one thing regarding mother's kitchen, however, I was certain—and that was that there was always plenty of food there, at least those classified as carbohydrates—plantain, yam, cocoyam, cassava, maize, etc.

In Mpintimpi, at the latest by eight in the morning, the first meal of the day—boiled plantain to go with *nkotomire* (leaves from the cocoyam plant) stew—was ready. It was followed about four hours later, most likely, with more boiled plantain and sauce made from garden eggs (vegetables found in Ghana). Not long thereafter, mother set about to prepare fufu.

The situation was very different when compared to the meals provided by my hosts. They seemed to have problems even with the basics—plantains, yams, cocoyams. Usually they had to wait till late in the morning—towards midday—to break their fast. Nothing usually followed thereafter till the evening meal. Not only that, the quantity of food served was meagre, nowhere near what I was used to!

My hosts seemed to have very limited cultivated farmland, and that was far removed from the borders of the town; I had to walk the long distance with them to visit the farmland. Initially I tried to suppress my tears. Soon I could no longer do so. In the end some members of the household noticed the problem and reported the matter to my big friend.

Initially, he tried to cheer me up—to no avail. In the end he was forced to cut short his stay by a few days and return to his post. As might be expected, I was overjoyed on stepping back on the soil of my beloved village.

--63--
"EYES ARE RED WHEN THINGS ARE BAD!"

I WAS BARELY SEVEN YEARS OLD when news began to spread in our little community to the effect that the *wansam* had arrived in the village!

Before I proceed, I shall pause for a while to shed some light on the term *wansam*. These were middle-aged men, usually from a tribe in Northern Ghana, who had mastered the art of circumcision (please do not ask me how!) and travelled round the country, especially the rural areas, to carry out circumcision on boys. Two factors came together to make the services of the *wansam* sought after in our community.

In the first place, the practice of male circumcision is well established in the tribe of the Akans, to which the overwhelming majority of the residents of the village belonged. Indeed, from time immemorial it has been customary for them to circumcise their boys. The only exemption from the rule involved the royals, especially those directly in line to the thrones. They were not circumcised, so it is reasoned, in order to spare them the excruciating pain involved in the process. It should be stressed at this juncture that female circumcision is not practised by the Akans.

The services of the *wansam* were also sought after for financial reasons—it was cheaper for parents to have their children circumcised by the *wansam* than to take them to the hospital in Nkawkaw. One might also mention the matter of convenience. How could the parents involved conveniently transport their children back to the village once they had undergone the procedure at Nkawkaw?

The news of the *wansam's* arrival in the area was soon verified. Since his arrival was a rare event, those parents whose boys were yet to be circumcised took advantage of the opportunity to get their boys through the ritual.

That happened to be the opportunity my own parents were also awaiting for, for three of their boys, the composer of this report as well as his two older brothers, were yet to have their foreskins removed. And so our parents registered the three of us with the visiting 'urologist'.

In the end, the 'surgeon' decided to make our makeshift bathroom his operating theatre, not only for the boys of that house, but also for several others in the village.

As far as the boys of my parents were concerned, Kwaku, who is five years my senior, was the first to face the 'baptism of fire'. He withstood the procedure, conducted without any form of anaesthesia, with bravado. Next on the 'surgical list' for the day was Kwame, who is two years my senior. When one of the 'surgical assistants' went to fetch him from the 'waiting room' he was nowhere to be found—he had vanished into thin air! A search was immediately conducted for him—to no avail. The 'surgeon' could not wait for him—the 'surgical list' for the day was long.

Next yours truly was called to the 'battlefield'. Although several years have elapsed since then, the sharp pain resulting from the severance of the foreskin is still firmly engraved on my brain! So also is the sight of blood gushing from the wound and the screams that ensued from my barely seven-year-old throat! Out of desperation, I made a frantic attempt to free myself from the ordeal—but there was no way of escape. Mr *Wansam* was not conducting the procedure alone; he was assisted by four well-built men, each holding firmly to one of my limbs!

Wherever he learnt his trade, he did in my opinion learn it well. The urologist, the doctor who has specialised in that area of medical practice, will tell you that severing the foreskin is not the end of the matter; one has to, as it were, tidy the area so as to obtain optimal results. That was exactly what the *wansam* did after he had cut the foreskin. In all, it took the 'expert' a good half an hour to complete his job, the 'victim' of the extraordinary surgical procedure for the most part crying at the top of his voice.

At long last, the relieving words: "It is done, carry him away!" emanated from his throat. With profuse sweat pouring from my body, I was helped onto a piece of cloth spread on the floor of our room.

In all, about a dozen boys in the small village underwent the procedure on that day. Over the next several days, a visitor to our village might have wondered why several boys on the street were moving about in a peculiar manner, as if they had something concealed between their legs that was impairing their movement.

Kwame returned from his hideout late in the evening. One day, several months later, probably as a result of the taunts from his peers who saw his 'problem' whenever we went to swim in the Nwi River, he got hold of a piece of chalk and wrote boldly on the wall of our room: "Eyes are red when things are bad."

About three years on, he was again brought before a *wansam* who had made a stop in the village. On this occasion he may well have drawn strength from his own words: "Eyes are red when things are bad"—for he prevailed and conquered his fears.

--64--
THE VILLAGE BOY GOES TO TOWN

AT THE BEGINNING OF 1971, I applied to sit the common entrance examination. A pass in it was a prerequisite for admission to a secondary school. Admission to a secondary school opened the door to several opportunities in one's academic career, including a possible admission to university.

He who could not make it into the secondary school could complete the ten-year elementary education with the so-called standard seven certificate (also known as middle school leaving certificate) and end up as a clerk or factory hand or, indeed, find himself unemployed.

The children of the middle class, the affluent and the rich, generally referred to in Ghana as *Dadamma* (Dada's children), alluding to the fact that such children call their fathers 'Dada', were usually sent to special primary schools, where they were groomed specially to pass the common entrance examination. These schools became known as preparatory schools.

The sons and daughters of ordinary citizens—impoverished peasants, fishermen, factory hands, the likes of Papa Kofi Gyamfi and Maame Amma Owusua of Mpintimpi, known in society as *Agyamma* (Agya's children) because they referred to their fathers as 'Agya' instead of 'Dada', on the other hand, attended the public elementary schools. Hardly any child there attempted the common entrance exam until they reached middle form 3 or form 4, corresponding to nine and ten years of elementary school education respectively.

Even then the pass rate for candidates from the elementary school was low compared to those from the preparatory school. Whereas some preparatory schools boasted a pass rate of over 95 per cent, even 100 per cent, the chance of a candidate from the elementary school passing the important test was very low indeed. In our case, out of about forty candidates who attempted the test only two were successful.

It was one thing passing the entrance examination, but another thing finding the needed sponsorship. Though, as mentioned elsewhere, tuition at that time was free from the elementary school up to university, many of the secondary schools were boarding schools. Whereas the rich might have considered the boarding and lodging fees just peanuts, to the ordinary citizen the fees amounted to a fortune.

To help cocoa farmers send their children to such schools, the CMB set up a scholarship scheme to cater for their children. At least that was what they were officially set up for. It was an open secret, however, that many a person of influence, some of whom had no idea what a cocoa tree even looked like (and besides, could afford to pay for their children's education without outside help), used their influence to acquire the scholarships for their children, to the detriment of those for whom it was really intended.

There was another hurdle in the way of the child of the cocoa farmer aspiring to win the CMB sponsorship. The scholarships were usually awarded on the basis of the results of the first few terms' examinations at the secondary school. In other words, one had to be already admitted into the secondary school to stand the chance of being sponsored by the CMB. How could the poor farmer come up with the initial funding?

Much credit goes to our parents, who braved all the financial odds to pay for the secondary school education of their second child, Ransford. It was a laudable decision on their part. It would lead the family into considerable financial problems for the most part of his five-year stay at the boarding school.

I profited from my parents' decision to pay for Ransford's education, notwithstanding that at the time I passed the common entrance examination several years later they were not in a position to sponsor me—owing to several other financial commitments.

Ransford, who had in the meantime entered the Ghana Air Force, decided to pay for my education! It was a bold decision on his part for which I am eternally grateful. Though I was granted a CMB scholarship shortly after my admission, without his initial sacrifice my educational career would have taken a different course.

On Thursday 16th September 1971, I joined a vehicle filled almost to the last seat bound for Akim Oda. With the "Do not forget us" departing words of the woman I referred to at the beginning of my narration still ringing in my ears, I embarked on the journey that would mark a defining moment in my life—indeed, that would mark the end of my almost uninterrupted stay in the little village.

Moving from Mpintimpi to the boarding school was like moving from the middle of the jungle into a booming modern city. All of a sudden, I was privileged to enjoy the luxury of living with electricity and all the other facilities associated with it—electric fans to cool our classrooms and dormitories, TV, electric irons, etc.

No longer would I walk barefoot along the streets of Mpintimpi and elsewhere—yes, barefoot on the burning hot ground heated by the scorching African sun. Even if I wanted to, I was not permitted. The boarding school had sent us a list of items I needed to purchase and these included what was described as 'cross- sandals' as well as a pair of black shoes.

Among the items we were asked to bring to the boarding school were toothbrush and toothpaste. Instead of resorting to chewing sticks the likes of *tweapea* and *nsorkodua* to clean my teeth, I was now expected to use a toothbrush and toothpaste.

Also, I was no longer permitted to eat with my fingers, at least not during the three daily gatherings of the whole school at the dining hall for the standard three meals of the day. To that end, the school asked us to purchase a set of cutlery.

How did someone who throughout his previous life was accustomed to eating with his 'natural set of cutlery' become conversant with eating with a spoon, a fork and a knife?

The school was not unaware of the difficulties faced by newcomers like me who hailed from *nhabamamu* (the bush), a term we were taunted with by our classmates from the cities—classmates whose duty it was to become our mentors to help us overcome the hurdle of our unsophisticated upbringing.

Our mentors taught us not only how to use the set of cutlery, but also how to put on a tie! Indeed, putting on the tie was also a duty! By the time the first Sunday evening church service came around, everyone, including the village boy from little Mpintimpi, had to be conversant with tying a tie, otherwise one risked being scolded by the house prefect, whose duty it was to make sure everyone in his dormitory had put on his white trousers, white shirt, a tie and a white coat for the church service, which was compulsory for all.

After almost twelve weeks' stay, I returned to Mpintimpi for the Christmas holidays. My stay had refined me, but not changed me. Though life would not be the same as before, I still accompanied my parents to the farm and enjoyed the company of my brother Kwame, who I had left behind, as well as my good friends Moses and Anorkwaah.

If moving into the boarding school refined me, it was growing up at Mpintimpi that formed my life, and for that I am eternally grateful to my little village. Being raised under those challenging conditions has helped me master almost any challenge that has come my way in life. Is it want? What is want when one has already learnt to live with almost nothing at Mpintimpi?!

Is it stress? What is stress when as a six-year-old I have had to get up early in the morning, walk to the Nwi River to fetch water, walk two miles to school, stay there all day without adequate meals, walk another two miles back home to help my parents prepare the evening meal before retiring to bed?

I have heard people say things like: "Don't get on my nerves!" Get on my nerves? What is provocation or 'getting on one's nerves' when as a child one lived with flies that settled on one's open wound, irritating it with bites? Or, to add insult to injury, was plagued by mosquitoes that, in the middle of the night, not only inflicted painful bites but would send one almost mad by way of their high-pitched buzzing?

Was it the threat of depression? I was exposed to so many heartbreaking situations during my life at Mpintimpi that I have grown immune to situations that might plummet others into depression!

It is true that events in my later life, especially my conversion to Christianity, have played a significant role in shaping my life. Without any doubt, however, Mpintimpi has had a lasting influence on me. It has, among other things, taught me humility, resilience, compassion, respect for the elderly, learning to share with others; for that I will be eternally grateful to the little village situated about 120 kilometres to the north of Accra, a few degrees north of the Equator.

--65--
DO NOT FORGET US STILL

DO NOT FORGET US...
Those words are still echoing in my ears…

Though owing to financial constraints, I have not been able to realise my vision of helping to raise the standard of the village, like setting up a clinic to cater for them, I have not in any way forgotten the lot of 'my people', the inhabitants of the little village I was privileged to grow up in.

Indeed, what I am doing at the moment, namely sitting down behind my desk in the middle of the night, trying to recollect my thoughts in an attempt to bring the plight of those village dwellers to the attention of the world, I consider as part of my commitment to that cause. If the narration in this book leads someone, somewhere, to contribute to the improvement of the lot of not only the poverty-stricken folk of Mpintimpi, but also that of the poor and destitute elsewhere in the world, my task will not have been in vain.

EPILOGUE
GHANA 2 USA 1

ON THE DAY GHANA BEAT THE USA 2–1 in the 2010 Football World Cup staged in South Africa, I made a mobile phone call to Manu, my sister in Mpintimpi.

"We are still celebrating Ghana's victory over the US", she said. "It was a great game!"

"Did you watch it?"

"Yes, GBC TV showed it live."

"You mean you have your own TV?"

"Yes—one of our relatives gave me one recently!"

"Is that the only TV set in the village?"

"No, several households have their own sets!"

Imagine being able to watch the World Cup live at Mpintimpi!? My eyes went back to the Football World Cup final between Holland and Germany in 1974! On that occasion, my brothers and I had to go round the village looking for a transistor radio so we could follow the commentary. Eventually we spotted one and were permitted to hang around to listen as Germany beat Holland 2–1 to lift the World Cup.

Now thirty-six years on, Mpintimpi seemed to have moved on. The impression is deceptive, however. Without doubt, the standard of living of the villagers, compared to the conditions I grew up in, has improved. In particular, the village has benefited from the national electrification programme begun in the early 1990s and which has the goal of providing electricity to as many places in the country as possible.

Our small settlement might have been overlooked had it not been for its location on the major trunk road I referred to at the beginning of this book. The foresight of our forefathers seemed, as it were, to be yielding dividends. As the story goes, initially the village was built near the Nwi River. Soon they realised they had not reckoned with the rains that set in at regular intervals to cause the river to overflow its banks, and into people's dwellings.

Eventually they decided to move to settle in an area about half a mile away. Just when they were about to settle down word reached them that the Government was about to construct a trunk road to link Akim Oda and Nkawkaw. First they rejoiced, thinking the road would pass through the village. Soon they were disappointed, for it passed about half a mile away.

No, we won't accept that, they resolved! If the road will not come to us, we will go to the road! That turned out to be a very important decision, for though small, the fact of the road brought several advantages, including the benefits that came from the national electrification project.

It could not be ignored, for the newly constructed electric line linking the two major towns referred to above, passed along the fringes of the village. Eventually an extension was made to the village, permitting those who could afford it to be supplied with electricity. Nevertheless, though electricity is available in theory, the hard realities of life there have forced the majority of residents to continue to rely on the kerosene lamps that helped me do my homework.

As far as the water supply is concerned, though there is still no pipe-borne water, the village has profited from the Government's water well-drilling programme. The village has a few wells, operated with hand-pumping machines. The quality of the water is generally said to be good, since the wells are unlike the well that we used to drink from. These new wells are completely covered, eliminating one important source of pollution.

That is where the light in the dark tunnel ends. The population still remains impoverished, still relying on the meagre income they obtain from selling their cocoa and occasionally from the surplus foodstuffs harvested from their fields.

www.ingramcontent.com/pod-product-compliance
Lightning Source LLC
Chambersburg PA
CBHW060515090426
42735CB00011B/2235